S0-ARN-445

Study Guide and Student Workbook

for use with

Music: An Appreciation

Fourth Edition

Roger Kamien
Hebrew University

Prepared by
Raoul F. Camus
Emeritus Professor, Queensborough Community College

McGraw Hill

Boston Burr Ridge, IL Dubuque, IA Madison, WI New York San Francisco St. Louis
Bangkok Bogotá Caracas Kuala Lumpur Lisbon London Madrid Mexico City
Milan Montreal New Delhi Santiago Seoul Singapore Sydney Taipei Toronto

McGraw-Hill Higher Education

A Division of The **McGraw-Hill** *Companies*

Study Guide and Student Workbook for use with
MUSIC: AN APPRECIATION, FOURTH EDITION
Kamien

Published by McGraw-Hill, an imprint of the McGraw-Hill Companies, Inc., 1221 Avenue of the Americas, New York, NY 10020. Copyright © 2002, 1998, 1994, 1990 by the McGraw-Hill Companies, Inc. All rights reserved.

No part of this publication may be reproduced or distributed in any form or by any means, or stored in a database or retrieval system, without the prior written consent of The McGraw-Hill Companies, Inc., including, but not limited to, in any network or other electronic storage or transmission, or broadcast for distance learning.

4 5 6 7 8 9 0 2 QPD/2QPD 0 9 8 7 6 5 4

ISBN 0-07-245765-1

www.mhhe.com

CONTENTS

IV. THE CLASSICAL PERIOD

V. THE ROMANTIC PERIOD

VII. NONWESTERN MUSIC

APPENDIX

TO THE STUDENT

This *Study Guide and Student Workbook* is designed to accompany Roger Kamien's *MUSIC: An Appreciation*, fourth brief edition, on which it is based. As the title indicates, this manual has two basic purposes:

1. The *Study Guide* is designed to help you in your preparation for class by reviewing the materials in the text through lists of "Basic Terms" and through "Self-Tests" consisting of multiple-choice, matching, or fill-in questions.

2. The *Student Workbook* contains exercises, research projects, and worksheets. Some are explorative, some argumentative, but all are designed to encourage thought and interaction in and outside of class. These pages may be used for

- classroom discussion
- listening or written assignments
- broadening the scope of understanding music in its relationship to the cultural periods and the other humanities
- reviewing the biographical details of some of the major composers and performers
- supplementing topics discussed in the text

SUGGESTIONS FOR USING THE STUDY GUIDE

The text on which this work is based is divided into seven major parts, with eighty sections. Most likely, the course you are taking will not cover all these sections because of time limitations, so you can use the Contents as a course outline by checking off those topics that will be covered. After reading an assignment, answer the questions in the Study Guide. Then, check your answers against those given in the back of this book. Reread the text, if necessary, for any questions that might still be unresolved.

At the end of each of the major units (corresponding to parts I through VII in the text), there is a unit quiz. Since the answers to the quiz questions are not given in this manual, the quizzes may be used by the instructor for review in class, for outside assignment, or for collection. If your instructor does not plan to use the unit quizzes in this way, please ask him or her to provide you with a photocopy of the answer page from the Instructor's Manual, so that you may do the work and check it on your own.

The text and accompanying materials have been designed to help you develop an understanding and appreciation of music, including different artistic styles and historical periods, something that can provide you with a lifelong source of pleasure, inspiration, and cultural enrichment. We sincerely hope you will give them a chance to do so, and we hope you will enjoy the time you spend in discovering that, like "reading, 'riting, and 'rithmetic," *Music is Basic!*

INTRODUCTION TO TECHNOLOGY
by Rebecca Kaufman

The world of technology has but one constant—it's always changing! New developments and technologies come out at a dizzying pace, making us wonder if we can keep up or should even try. Computer software can present information, provide out-of-class drills, establish a creative environment, or encourage the development of problem-solving skills. It can enhance our learning efforts in creative and effective ways, if we understand how it can work for us.

Technology also includes the mysterious realm of cyberspace, i.e., the Internet and the World Wide Web. What is to be gained by entering the "information superhighway?" For one thing, we can access information that used to be inaccessible or very difficult to pursue, such as rare music manuscripts or research materials. We can also connect with new sources of current information and establish contact with others in our areas of interest. We can listen to or download music files for instant sound through the computer without an instrument or CD player. Last, but not least, we can explore or "surf" the World Wide Web for fun. It's a big information world out there. We can take in as little or as much as we want. But to do so, we must be explorers, ready to jump on board and go along for the ride, learning as we go. To be willing to learn new things is a valuable skill in the information age.

Once a common network language for computers was developed in 1969, computers could be linked together and the Internet was born. In 1991, a graphical user interface with icons and images gave rise to the World Wide Web (WWW), or Web for short. Information from the Web can be in the form of text, images, sounds, or movies.

To gain access to the Web, there are some basic requirements: 1) a computer with at least 8 MB of RAM (preferably more); 2) a modem (the faster the better) and an account with an Internet service provider or a direct Internet connection via your school; and 3) software to access the Internet.

The Web can be accessed with a *browser*, which is software that acts as a gateway to the Web. The browser on your computer contacts another computer and sets up the link. It then displays the information it receives on your computer screen. The technical terms for this arrangement are *client* and *server*. The client is your computer, which requests information, and the server is the computer that provides that information. Your browser contacts a server via its address, much like regular mail. This address is called a URL, or universal resource locator. This is a sample URL: **http://www.mhhe.com**. To make it easier to read and avoid confusion, from here on all URLs, or parts of URLs, will be enclosed in angle brackets, but the angle brackets are not part of the URL:

< http://www.mhhe.com >

This URL contains several parts. The first few characters, < http:// >, are the protocol and you will see them at the beginning of all Web URLs. Other older but still active protocols include < ftp:// > and < gopher:// >. The actual server is listed next, in this case, < www.mhhe >. Many Web addresses begin with < www. >. At the end of the URL is < .com >. This is the domain, which gives you a clue as to the type of server. Some common domains are *.com* for commercial, *.edu* for an educational institution, *.gov* for government, *.mil* for military, and *.org* for organization. Foreign sites have an additional letter code at the end of the domain, such as *.au* for Australia, *.nl* for Netherlands, and *.uk* for the United Kingdom. Each character must be correct in a URL or the link won't be established. If you have access to the Web, test the waters by visiting the McGraw-Hill site at < http://www.mhhe.com >. Once you are there, see if you can find your way to a citation of this book or a reference to Roger Kamien. What did you have to do to find the information? Although Web sites can be organized differently, there are many similarities among them.

How do we get URLs? Perhaps someone has given you a URL to check out or you have noticed a URL as part of a company's advertisement. You can visit that site by typing in the correct URL in your browser's entry line, called the GoTo line. To find sites without knowing the URL, you can use a directory or a search engine. A directory lists categories of information, categories that become more detailed as selections are made. If you feel like browsing, use a directory. If you want something specific, use a search engine. With a search engine, you may enter one or several keywords and let the search engine find possible matches. Because of the dynamic nature of the Web, to stay current it makes sense to do fresh searches each time you want specific information.

To do effective searches on the Web, it helps to know what makes for a good search. Each search engine does a search a bit differently, so take the time to read their tips for successful searches. A general search for "music" might return 800,000 sites (called "hits" in Web terminology). It doesn't make sense to wade through 800,000 hits to find the perfect crumhorn site. Again, if you want to browse, use a directory. For a specific search, use restrictors, such as AND, NOT, and OR. The presence of the restrictor AND, or a plus sign (+) in some search engines, as in "Mozart AND clarinet," searches for sites that contain both terms. The restrictor NOT, or a minus sign (-), eliminates certain sites and tightens up the search. The restrictor OR increases the number of hits by including all sites that mention either of the terms used in the search. AND and NOT will benefit you the most in the long run. For practice, check out the Infoseek Ultra search engine at **< http://ultra.infoseek.com >** and do a search with these keywords: + Clara Schumann, + Johannes Brahms (this is the correct format for an Infoseek Ultra search). The search engine will find all sites with both names mentioned. See if you can find a site that follows the correspondence between the two composers. How would you refine the search even more if all you wanted was the correspondence? Each search engine takes practice to learn, so be patient and experiment with how you use keywords. Keep refining your search parameters until you have a short list of sites. To avoid searching with several search engines, you might want to try a metasearch, which is one service searching with several search engines and posting all of the results. The table of URLs below lists a number of search engines and some popular metasearch sites.

At the heart of the Web is the Web *page*, which is the primary medium for information. A Web page is what you see when you connect with a site. A Web page displays information, but its most important feature is *hypermedia*, or links to other web pages on other computers. *Hypertext* is text in a different color or underlined, which means you can click on the text to go to another Web page. Pictures can be also be links, such as a map that lets you zoom in on a particular area through a series of clicks and end up at a site with relevant tourist information. English is the most common language on the Web, but there are other languages, too.

Because the Web depends on connections between computers and Web traffic is increasing rapidly, interruptions happen frequently. If your request to connect with a site is rejected or doesn't go through, try again later. If a page starts to load but doesn't finish or you see the message "transfer interrupted," reload the page from your browser's options. Be persistent and patient.

Once you start exploring, it's easy to get lost and forget where you started or where you were headed. Luckily, the browser keeps track of the sites visited and you can retrace your steps either through the Go menu, which lists the most recent sites visited, or the Back and Forward buttons, which let you step back and forward through your most recent sites. You can set up bookmarks at your favorite sites so that it is easy to return to them, but keep in mind that bookmarks need to be updated, too. Return visits to favorite sites can yield valuable new information and new links to other sites. A well-maintained Web site with updated links to specific sites is your best bet to stay current. Chances are the technology you discover will spur you on to further explorations. The table below lists some good sites from which to start your exploring. In the parlance of the Web, happy surfing!

TABLE OF URLS

Site Name	Description	URL
Internet Tutorials		
Learn the Net	tutorial and information in four languages	http://www.learnthenet.com
Help Web	guide to getting started on the Internet	http://www.imagescape.com/helpweb
Internet Web Text	hypertext guide to Internet resources	http://www.december.com/web/text
Search Engines		
AltaVista	for simple and advanced searches	http://www.altavista.digital.com
Lycos	thorough search of Internet by keyword	http://www.lycos.com
Magellan Internet Guide	search engine plus four-star rating system	http://magellan.excite.com
MetaCrawler	parallel search with nine services	http://www.metacrawler.com
ProFusion	design-your-own metasearch	http://www.profusion.com
SavvySearch	detailed search with 28+ search engines	http://www.search.com
WebCrawler	detailed search by keyword	http://www.webcrawler.com
Yahoo	subject-oriented directory	http://www.yahoo.com
Music Resources		
Worldwide Internet Music Resources	directory of music resources links	http://www.music.indiana.edu/music_resources
Internet Resources for Music Scholars	research directory	http://www.rism.harvard.edu/MusicLibrary/InternetResources.html
Music Resources from the Sibelius Academy	extensive lists of music sites	http://www.siba.fi:80/Kulttuuripalvelut/music.html
WWW Virtual Library	music directory and alphabetical index	http://www.gprep.org/classical
Classical Net Home Page	index and links to classical music sites	http://www.classical.efront.com
MUSIClassical.com	links to various music sites	http://www.angelfire.com/biz/musiclassical/index.html
Bringing American Music Home	guide for teachers of music history	http://falcon.cc.ukans.edu/~bclark/groubody.html
Historic American Sheet Music	index and illustrations of sheet music	http://scriptorium.lib.duke.edu/sheetmusic
Dance Resources		
American Ballet Theatre	repertory archives, photos, dictionary	http://abt.org
American Ballroom Companion	dance instruction manuals, c1490-1920	http:memory.loc.gov/ammem/dihtml/dihome.html
Dance Heritage Coalition	tutorial for in-depth dance research	http://www.danceheritage.org
Music Organizations		
College Music Society	info and links to resources	http://www.music.org
American Musicological Society	info and links to musicological sites	http://www.ams-net.org
Recording Companies		
BMG Classics World	catalog of releases, classical music guides	http://www.getmusic.com/classical/bmg
Sony Online	catalog of Sony products and ventures	http://www.sony.com
Other Sites of Interest		
WebMuseum	catalog of art works for display	http://SunSITE.sut.ac.jp/wm/
Classical MIDI Archives	many classical MIDI files	http://www.prs.net/midi.html
MIDI Farm	directory of MIDI files	http://www.midifarm.com/directory.htm
Classical Composers Archive	small pictures and brief biographies	http://spight.physics.unlv.edu/picgalr2.htm
Library of Congress	LoC online resources	http://lcweb.loc.gov

Name_____ Class/section_____ Date_____

PRE-COURSE Class: ___Freshman ___Sophomore ___Junior ___Senior ___Graduate
QUESTIONNAIRE Major:_____ Minor:_____

Technology: I ___ do ____ do not have a computer. I ____ do ____ do not have access to the Internet.

Background in music:
  Junior high school: ___none ___general music course
    ___performing group:_____
  High school: ___none ___general music course ___theory ___other
    ___chorus (voice:_____) ___stage band/combo
    ___band ___orchestra (instrument:_____)
  College courses: ___none ___survey/appreciation ___theory
    ___performing group:_____ (instrument:_____)
  Private lessons: ___none ___years of piano ___years of _____

Reason for taking the present course (check as many as apply):
  ____college requirement for degree program
  ____personal enrichment
  ____recommended by advisor
  ____only class I could fit into my program
  ____other:_____

Musical habits:
  I attend about _____ concerts per _____, most of which are _____(style)
  I listen to about _____ hours per _____ of music on the radio, most of which
    is _____ (style), on station(s) _____
  I buy about _____ cassettes/CDs per _____, most of which are _____(style)

I have had the following musical experiences:

	PERFORMER OR WORK	WHEN	REACTION
ballet	_____	_____	_____
chamber music	_____	_____	_____
chorus or choir	_____	_____	_____
jazz group	_____	_____	_____
opera or musical	_____	_____	_____
recital	_____	_____	_____
rock group	_____	_____	_____
stage band	_____	_____	_____
symphonic band	_____	_____	_____
symphonic orchestra	_____	_____	_____
other: _____	_____	_____	_____

Preferences in music:

My favorite musical compositions are:
  TITLE   COMPOSER
1. _____   _____
2. _____   _____
3. _____   _____

My favorite composers are:
1. _____
2. _____
3. _____

My favorite performers are:
  INDIVIDUALS   GROUPS
1. _____   _____
2. _____   _____
3. _____   _____

Identify and describe in your own words the following musical styles:

baroque: _____

blues: _____

classical: _____

jazz: _____

rap: _____

rock: _____

romantic: _____

Define the following musical terms:

pitch: _____

dynamics: _____

harmony: _____

melody: _____

rhythm: _____

tempo: _____

timbre: _____

What do you hope to achieve, other than the necessary credit, from this course?

I. ELEMENTS

I-1. SOUND: PITCH, DYNAMICS, AND TONE COLOR

BASIC TERMS:

sound	interval	dynamics
pitch	octave	accent
tone	pitch range (range)	tone color (timbre)

SELF-TEST Multiple-choice: Circle the answer that best completes each item.

1. *Timbre* is synonymous with
   a. sound
   b. vibrations
   c. tone color
   d. dynamic accent

2. Degrees of loudness and softness in music are called
   a. dynamics
   b. pitches
   c. notes
   d. tone colors

3. The relative highness or lowness of a sound is called
   a. timbre
   b. pitch
   c. dynamics
   d. octave

4. The distance between the lowest and highest tones that a voice or instrument can produce is called
   a. pitch range
   b. an octave
   c. timbre
   d. dynamic accent

5. The Italian dynamic markings traditionally used to indicate very soft, loud, and very loud are (respectively)
   a. piano, mezzo forte, forte
   b. mezzo piano, forte, fortissimo
   c. pianissimo, piano, forte
   d. pianissimo, forte, fortissimo

6. The pitch of a sound is decided by the _____ of its vibrations.
   a. amplitude
   b. timbre
   c. frequency
   d. dynamics

7. The distance in pitch between any two tones is called
   a. duration
   b. dynamic accent
   c. timbre
   d. an interval

8. When two different tones blend so well when sounded together that they almost seem to merge into one tone, the interval is called a(n)
   a. dynamic accent
   b. octave
   c. interval
   d. pitch range

9. The frequency of vibrations is measured in
   a. cycles per minute
   b. cycles per second
   c. dynamic levels
   d. Italian words

10. A dynamic accent occurs in music when a performer
    a. emphasizes a tone by playing it more loudly than the tones around it
    b. plays all the notes loudly
    c. stamps his or her foot on the floor
    d. begins speeding up the music

11. A gradual increase in loudness is known as a
    a. decrescendo   c. fortissimo
    b. crescendo   d. diminuendo

12. In music, a sound that has a definite pitch is called a
    a. noise   c. sound
    b. dynamic accent   d. tone

13. The symbol ⟍⟋ indicates to the performer that the music should
    a. gradually increase in loudness   c. gradually decrease in loudness
    b. gradually decrease in pitch   d. be played faster

14. Music can be defined as
    a. sounds produced by musical instruments
    b. sounds that are pleasing, as opposed to noise
    c. an art based on the organization of sounds in time
    d. a system of symbols which performers learn to read

15. In general, the smaller the vibrating element, the _____ its pitch.
    a. higher   c. lower
    b. softer   d. louder

LISTENING EXERCISE   Pitch discrimination: Some people believe they are monotones, unable to sing on pitch or tell one piece of music from another. It is very rare that this is true, but there are individual differences in the ability to discriminate pitches. Just as we learn through practice to differentiate colors with our eyes, we can develop pitch differentiation.

To see how well you can hear pitch differences, try the following exercise. The instructor will play two pitches in succession (or you can ask a friend to do this outside of class). Is the second pitch higher, lower, or the same as the first? Check your responses.

1. ____higher   ____lower   ____unison   ____octave
2. ____higher   ____lower   ____unison   ____octave
3. ____higher   ____lower   ____unison   ____octave
4. ____higher   ____lower   ____unison   ____octave
5. ____higher   ____lower   ____unison   ____octave
6. ____higher   ____lower   ____unison   ____octave
7. ____higher   ____lower   ____unison   ____octave
8. ____higher   ____lower   ____unison   ____octave
9. ____higher   ____lower   ____unison   ____octave
10. ____higher   ____lower   ____unison   ____octave

LISTENING EXERCISE   Timbres—Tone colors and combinations:

Just as pitch discrimination can be developed through practice, so too can one develop the ability to recognize the sounds of the various instruments and their combinations. To see how well you can recognize individual voice ranges or instruments, identify them in each of ten excerpts played in class.

1.

2.

3.

4.

5.

6.

7.

8.

9.

10.

LISTENING EXERCISE   Timbres—Performing media:

To see how well you can recognize combinations of sounds in their normal groupings, identify the medium—such as orchestra, band, rock group, jazz combo, or chorus—of each of ten excerpts played in class.

1.

2.

3.

4.

5.

6.

7.

8.

9.

10.

PRE-COURSE LISTENING ANALYSIS

Listen to the **Prelude to Act III of Richard Wagner's** *Lohengrin*. Write your personal and emotional reactions to the work, and try to analyze the music and its technical aspects as completely and specifically as you can.

Now listen to *C-Jam Blues* as performed by Duke Ellington and his orchestra. Once again, write your personal and emotional reactions to the work, and try to analyze the music and its technical aspects as completely and specifically as you can, comparing it with the Wagner prelude.

I-2. PERFORMING MEDIA: VOICES AND INSTRUMENTS

BASIC TERMS:

Voices
- soprano
- mezzo-soprano
- alto (or contralto)
- tenor
- baritone
- bass

Musical Instruments
- register

String Instruments
- violin
- viola
- cello (violoncello)
- double bass
- bow
- pizzicato
- stop (double, triple, quadruple)
- vibrato
- mute
- tremolo
- harmonics
- plectrum (plectra)
- harp
- guitar

Woodwind Instruments
- piccolo
- flute
- recorder
- single-reed woodwinds
  - clarinet
  - bass clarinet
  - saxophone
- double-reed woodwinds
  - oboe
  - english horn
  - bassoon
  - contrabassoon

Brass Instruments
- trumpet
- cornet
- french horn (horn)
- trombone
- baritone horn
- euphonium
- tuba
- mute

Percussion Instruments: definite pitch
- timpani (kettledrums)
- glockenspiel
- xylophone
- celesta
- chimes

Percussion Instruments: indefinite pitch
- snare drum (side drum)
- bass drum
- tambourine
- triangle
- cymbals
- gong (tam-tam)

Keyboard Instruments
- piano
- harpsichord
- pipe organ
- accordion

Electronic Instruments
- tape studio
- synthesizer
- analog synthesis
- digital frequency modulation (FM) synthesis
- effects devices
- sampling
- musical instrument digital interface (MIDI)
- computer

SELF-TEST Multiple-choice: Circle the answer that best completes each item.

1. A thin piece of cane, used singly or in pairs by woodwind players, is called a
   a. reed
   b. mute
   c. double stop
   d. mouthpiece

2. The strings of a violin are tuned
   a. by moving the bridge
   b. by putting on new strings
   c. by tightening or loosening the pegs
   d. at the factory

3. The lowest instrument in the orchestra is the
   a. piccolo
   b. tuba
   c. double bass
   d. contrabassoon

4. Systems of electronic components that generate, modify, and control sound are called
   a. amplifiers
   b. computers
   c. synthesizers
   d. stereo sets

5. A part of an instrument's total range is called a
   a. mute
   b. register
   c. pizzicato
   d. range

6. It is difficult to sing well because _____ than in speaking.
   a. singing demands a greater supply and control of breath
   b. wider ranges of pitch and volume are used
   c. vowel sounds are held longer
   d. all of the above

7. The bow that string players usually use to produce sound on their instruments is a slightly curved stick strung tightly with
   a. catgut
   b. horsehair
   c. string
   d. flax

8. The highest woodwind instrument in the orchestra is the
   a. piccolo
   b. flute
   c. oboe
   d. clarinet

9. If a string player uses vibrato—rocking of the left hand to produce small pitch fluctuations—it is because
   a. using vibrato is easier than not using it, and no one can hear the fluctuations anyway
   b. the performer is nervous
   c. the performer is unsure of the correct pitch
   d. using vibrato makes the tone warmer and more expressive

10. Plucking the string with the finger instead of using a bow is called
    a. tremolo
    b. pizzicato
    c. vibrato
    d. pluckato

11. Symphonic bands differ from symphonic orchestras in that they
    a. are smaller
    b. have a drum major instead of a conductor
    c. play only marches
    d. do not contain a string section

12. A hollow, funnel-shaped piece of wood or plastic that brass players use to alter the tone of their instruments is called a
    a. tailpiece
    b. crook
    c. mute
    d. reed

13. Woodwind instruments are so named because they
    a. are made of wood
    b. use a wooden reed
    c. have wooden key mechanisms
    d. were originally made of wood

14. The range of a singer's voice depends on
    a. training
    b. physical makeup
    c. training and physical makeup
    d. which microphone the singer uses

15. The very high-pitched tones that are produced when a string player lightly touches certain points on a string are called
    a. harmonics
    b. vibrato
    c. pizzicato
    d. tremolo

16. The main tool of composers of electronic music during the 1950s was the
    a. synthesizer
    b. tape studio
    c. piano
    d. sampler

SELF-TEST Matching: Match each term with its definition.

17. analog synthesis

18. digital synthesis

19. MIDI

20. sampling

a. technology based on placing brief digital recordings of live sounds under the control of a synthesizer keyboard

b. technology based on representing data in terms of measurable physical quantities

c. a standard adopted by manufacturers for interfacing synthesizer equipment

d. technology based on representing physical quantitites as numbers

EXERCISE Voices and instruments: Complete the following charts by placing each voice or instrument listed in "Basic Terms" (page 5) in its proper place.

1. Voices and strings.

FAMILY	VOICE	STRING (CHORDOPHONES)	
VIBRATING ELEMENT:	Vocal chords	Stretched strings	
		BOWED	PLUCKED
PITCH RANGE: Sopranino			
Soprano			
Alto			
Tenor			
Baritone			
Bass			
Contrabass			
Exceptions			

2. Woodwinds and brasses.

WOODWIND (AEROPHONES)			BRASS (AEROPHONES)
VIBRATING ELEMENT: a vibrating column of air			Lips
WITHOUT A REED	SINGLE-REED	DOUBLE-REED	

3. Percussion Instruments:

STRETCHED MEMBRANE (MEMBRANOPHONES)	
DEFINITE PITCH	INDEFINITE PITCH

SELF-SOUNDING (IDIOPHONES)	
DEFINITE PITCH	INDEFINITE PITCH

4. Keyboard Instruments:

INSTRUMENT	VIBRATING ELEMENT	MANNER OF TONE PRODUCTION
piano		
harpsichord		
organ		
accordion		
synthesizer		

RESEARCH PROJECT Seating plans: Fill in the blank spaces as appropriate.

1. Your local professional orchestra.

Name of orchestra:_____

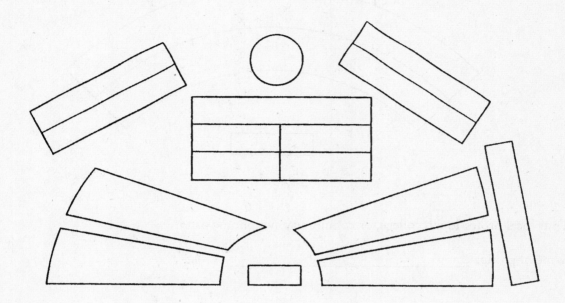

2. Your local college or community orchestra.

Name of orchestra: _____

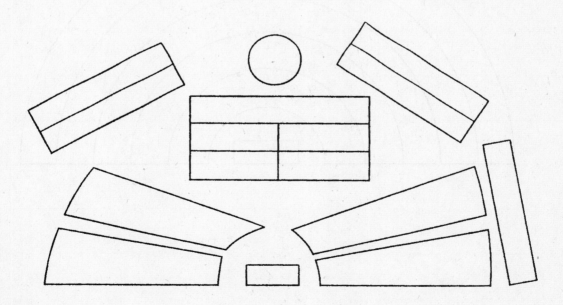

3. Your local college or community choir or choral society.

Name of group:_____

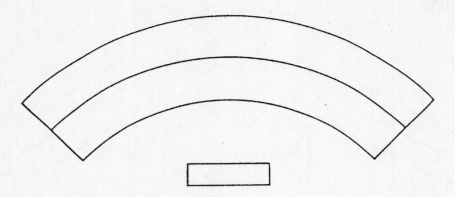

4. Your local professional, college, or community symphonic band.

Name of group: _____

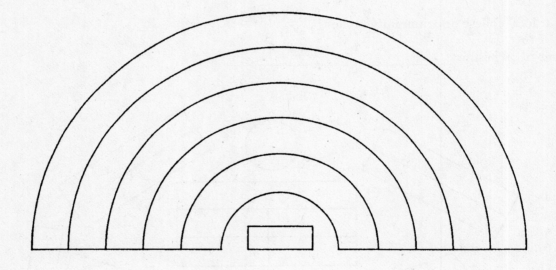

I-3. RHYTHM

BASIC TERMS:

beat	meter (duple, triple,	upbeat	tempo indication
rhythm	quadruple, quintuple,	accent	metronome
measure	sextuple, septuple)	syncopation	accelerando
	downbeat	tempo	ritardando

SELF-TEST Matching: Match each term with its description.

1. accent

2. beat

3. downbeat

4. measure

5. meter

6. metronome

7. rhythm

8. syncopation

9. tempo

10. upbeat

a. unit or group containing a fixed number of beats

b. organization of beats into regular groupings

c. stress or emphasis on a note

d. particular arrangement of note lengths in a piece of music; the ordered flow of music through time

e. putting an accent in music where it would not normally be expected

f. rate of speed of the beat of music

g. unaccented pulse preceding the downbeat

h. first, or stressed, beat of the measure

i. regular, recurrent pulsation that divides music into equal units of time

j. device that produces ticking sounds or flashes of light at any desired musical speed

MATCHING: Match each Italian tempo marking with its English translation.

11. accelerando
12. adagio
13. allegro
14. andante
15. largo
16. molto
17. non troppo
18. prestissimo
19. ritardando
20. vivace

k. as fast (quickly) as possible
l. very slow; broad
m. gradual speeding up of tempo
n. lively
o. slow
p. much
q. gradual slowing down of tempo
r. not too much
s. fast
t. moderately slow, a walking pace

I-4. MUSIC NOTATION

BASIC TERMS:

notation	natural sign (♮)	stem	tie
note	treble clef	flag	triplet
staff (staves)	bass clef	beam	rest
ledger lines	grand staff	dotted note	time (meter) signature
sharp sign (♯)	middle C	dotted rhythm	score
flat sign (♭)			

SELF-TEST Completion: Write the letter names of each of the notes in these measures:

1. __ __ __ __   2. __ __ __ __   3. __ __ __ __

4. __ __ __ __   5. __ __ __ __   6. __ __ __ __

EXERCISES Practice in notation:

1. Draw five treble and five bass clefs, copying the pattern.

2. Draw each of the accidental signs, following the examples.

3. Practice drawing whole notes by copying the C major scale.

4. Practice drawing notes by copying *The Farmer in the Dell* (see text).

5. Write three of each rest, following the examples in your text.

Whole rests   Half rests   Quarter rests   Eighth rests   Sixteenth rests

6. Some blank staves for practice, assignments, or original compositions:

I-5. MELODY

BASIC TERMS:

melody	legato	cadence
step	staccato	incomplete cadence
leap	phrase	complete cadence
climax	sequence	theme

SELF-TEST Multiple-choice: Circle the answer that best completes each item.

1. A melodic phrase ending that sets up expectations for continuation is known as a(n)
   a. incomplete cadence
   b. complete cadence
   c. sentence
   d. theme

2. A series of single tones that add up to a recognizable whole is called a
   a. cadence
   b. rhythm
   c. melody
   d. sequence

3. The emotional focal point of a melody is called the
   a. sequence
   b. theme
   c. cadence
   d. climax

4. The repetition of a melodic pattern at a higher or lower pitch is called a
   a. climax
   b. sequence
   c. cadence
   d. phrase

5. A resting place at the end of a phrase is called a
   a. climax
   b. melody
   c. stop
   d. cadence

6. A part of a melody is called a
   a. cadence
   b. sequence
   c. phrase
   d. step

7. *Legato* refers to playing or singing a melody
   a. in a short, detached manner
   b. in a smooth, connected style
   c. at a higher or lower pitch
   d. by small steps

8. A melody that serves as the starting point for a more extended piece of music is called a
   a. theme
   b. tune
   c. climax
   d. cadence

9. A melody is said to move by steps if it moves by
   a. repeating the same notes
   b. having rests between the notes
   c. large intervals
   d. adjacent scale tones

10. A short, detached style of playing a melody is known as
   a. legato
   b. staccato
   c. glissando
   d. vibrato

I-6. HARMONY

BASIC TERMS:

harmony	dissonance	dominant chord
chord	resolution	cadence
progression	triad	broken chord (arpeggio)
consonance	tonic chord	

SELF-TEST Multiple-choice: Circle the answer that best completes each item.

1. A combination of three or more tones sounded at the same time is called
   a. harmony   b. consonance   c. a chord   d. dissonance

2. *Harmony* refers to
   a. the way chords are constructed and how they follow each other
   b. living in peace with other people
   c. a pattern of beats per measure
   d. a chord built on the first step of the scale

3. The triad built on the fifth step of the scale is called the
   a. tonic chord   c. progression
   b. dominant chord   d. resolution

4. *Resolution* refers to a(n)
   a. dissonant chord moving to a consonant chord   c. composer resolving to write a composition
   b. consonant chord moving to a dissonant chord   d. arpeggio

5. _____ in music adds support, depth, and richness to a melody.
   a. rhythm   c. meter
   b. tempo   d. harmony

6. When the individual tones of a chord are sounded one after another instead of simultaneously,
   it is called a *broken chord* or
   a. cadence   c. allegro
   b. arpeggio   d. progression

7. A combination of tones that is considered unstable and tense is called a
   a. consonance   c. dissonance
   b. progression   d. chord

8. Traditionally, a composition would almost always end on a
   a. progression   c. dominant chord
   b. dissonant chord   d. tonic chord

9. A series of chords is called a(n)
   a. triad   c. arpeggio
   b. progression   d. consonance

10. A combination of tones that is considered stable and restful is called a
    a. consonance   b. dissonance   c. progression   d. chord

I-7. KEY

BASIC TERMS:

keynote (tonic)	key signature	chromatic scale
key (tonality)	half step	modulation
scale	whole step	tonic key (home key)
major scale	minor scale	

SELF-TEST Multiple-choice: Circle the answer that best completes each item.

1. *Key* refers to
   a. the major scale
   b. a central tone, chord, and scale
   c. any twelve random pitches
   d. a musical symbol placed at the beginning of the staff

2. Another term for *key* is
   a. tonality
   b. scale
   c. chromaticism
   d. dominant

3. In traditional western music, the _____ is the smallest interval between successive tones of a scale.
   a. quarter step
   b. whole step
   c. half step
   d. octave

4. A shift from one key to another within the same composition is called
   a. key
   b. resolution
   c. scale
   d. modulation

5. The central tone around which a musical composition is organized is called the
   a. scale
   b. dominant
   c. tonic
   d. modulation

EXERCISE Scales: Write the following scales (don't forget the clef):

G major   D major

Eb major   F major

D minor (harmonic form)   D minor (melodic form)

I-8. MUSICAL TEXTURE

BASIC TERMS:

musical texture	unison	counterpoint	homophonic texture
monophonic texture	polyphonic texture	imitation	

SELF-TEST Multiple-choice: Circle the answer that best completes each item.

1. *Musical texture* refers to
   a. how many different layers of sound are heard at the same time
   b. what kind of layers of sound are heard (melody or harmony)
   c. how layers of sound are related to each other
   d. all of the above

2. When a melodic idea is presented by one voice or instrument and then restated immediately by another voice or instrument, the technique is called
   a. counterpoint
   b. imitation
   c. copying
   d. all of the above

3. A *round* is an example of
   a. homophonic texture
   b. monophonic texture
   c. strict imitation
   d. sloppy singing

4. When there is one main melody accompanied by chords, the texture is
   a. polyphonic   b. homophonic   c. monophonic   d. imitative

5. The texture of a single melodic line without accompaniment is
   a. contrapuntal   b. homophonic   c. monophonic   d. polyphonic

6. Performance of a single melodic line by more than one instrument or voice is described as playing or singing in
   a. unison   b. counterpoint   c. harmony   d. imitation

7. The technique of combining several melodic lines into a meaningful whole is called
   a. texture   b. imitation   c. unison   d. counterpoint

8. An example of homophonic texture could be a
   a. hymn
   b. barbershop quartet
   c. folksinger accompanied by a guitar
   d. any of the above

9. When two or more melodic lines of equal interest are performed simultaneously, the texture is
   a. monophonic
   b. homophonic
   c. polyphonic
   d. heterophonic

10. *Contrapuntal texture* is sometimes used in place of the term
   a. monophonic texture
   b. homophonic texture
   c. polyphonic texture
   d. unisonal performance

I-9. MUSICAL FORM

BASIC TERMS:

form	contrast	three-part form (A B A)
repetition	variation	two-part form (A B)

SELF-TEST Multiple-choice: Circle the answer that best completes each item.

1. Retaining some features of a musical idea while changing others is called
   a. form   b. contrast   c. repetition   d. variation

2. Three-part form can be represented as
   a. A B A   c. statement, contrast, return
   b. A B A'   d. all of the above

3. The organization of musical ideas in time is called
   a. form   b. repetition   c. ternary   d. variation

4. Repetition is a technique widely used in music because it
   a. creates a sense of unity
   b. helps engrave a melody in the memory
   c. provides a feeling of balance and symmetry
   d. any of the above

5. The form consisting of a musical statement followed by a counterstatement would be called
   a. ternary   c. free
   b. binary   d. any of the above

LISTENING EXERCISE Listening for form:

As you listen to music, try to become aware of the form. Hum some old, familiar melodies, listen to the radio or television, or attend a concert, and list as many forms as you can recognize. Two examples are provided.

BINARY FORMS		TERNARY FORMS	
America	ab	*Home on the Range*	aa'ba'
_____		_____	
_____		_____	
_____		_____	
_____		_____	

I-10. MUSICAL STYLE

BASIC TERM:
style

SELF-TEST Multiple-choice: Circle the answer that best completes each item.

1. Which of the following would be a good example of a change in musical style?
   a. The men in the New York Philharmonic wear white tie and tails during the winter season, but for the summer concerts they wear black tie and white dinner jackets.
   b. The major and minor scales were the basic scales of western music from the 1600s to the 1900s, but in the twentieth century many composers abandoned tonality.
   c. The treble clef is used for relatively high pitch ranges, but the bass clef is used for lower ranges.
   d. all of the above.

2. Changes in musical style from one historical period to the next are usually
   a. continuous
   b. recognizable only by scholars and professional musicians
   c. very abrupt
   d. for the worse

3. We know little about the music of very ancient civilizations because
   a. there probably was almost none
   b. it was too primitive to interest later generations
   c. it is too difficult to be played today
   d. hardly any notated music has survived from these cultures

EXERCISE Stylistic periods:

Although there is no substitute for memorizing the styles and their approximate dates given in the textbook, the task will be easier if you associate each period with famous personalities; costume styles; dances; works of literature, art, and architecture; and historical and cultural events. Using the chart on the next page, make as many meaningful associations with each period as you can, and at the same time see how many musicians you can name. Some major events and personalities may be found in the textbook (see the Time-line for each stylistic period).

STYLISTIC PERIOD	Historical and Cultural Events	Famous Personalities	Musicians
Middle Ages (450-1450)			
Renaissance (1450-1600)			
Baroque (1600-1750)			
Classical (1750-1820)			
Romantic (1820-1900)			
Twentieth century to 1945			
1945 to the present			

Name_____

Class/section_____Date_____

Matching: Match each term with its definition:

a. cadence

b. chord

c. consonance

d. dissonance

e. dominant

f. dynamics

g. harmony

h. interval

i. melody

j. meter

k. modulation

l. phrase

m. pitch

n. rhythm

o. sequence

p. syncopation

q. tempo

r. theme

s. timbre

t. tonic

1. shifting from one key to another within a musical composition   1._____

2. tone color; quality of sound   2._____

3. stable combination of tones; points of rest   3._____

4. degrees of loudness and softness in music; intensity of sound   4._____

5. series of single tones that add up to a recognizable whole; musical sentence   5._____

6. distance in pitch between any two tones   6._____

7. chord built on the first step of the scale; central key around which a musical composition is organized   7._____

8. progression of chords leading to a feeling of repose at the end of a phrase; musical punctuation mark   8._____

9. repetition of a melodic pattern at a higher or lower pitch   9._____

10. relative highness or lowness of sound; frequency of vibrations   10._____

11. part of a melody   11._____

12. particular arrangement of note lengths in a piece of music; ordered flow of music through time   12._____

13. how chords are constructed and follow each other   13._____

14. combination of three or more tones sounded at the same time   14._____

15. placing an accent in music where it would not normally be expected   15._____

16. organization of beats into regular groupings; time signature   16._____

17. speed of a beat   17._____

18. triad built on the fifth step of the scale   18._____

19. melody that serves as the starting point for a more extended piece of music   19._____

20. unstable combination of tones; tension demanding onward motion   20._____

Unit Quiz I (cont.)

Matching: Match each instrument with its family grouping:

	21. trumpet	21._____
a. strings	22. saxophone	22._____
	23. cello	23._____
b. woodwinds	24. english horn	24._____
	25. vibraphone	25._____
c. brass	26. trombone	26._____
	27. violin	27._____
d. percussion	28. oboe	28._____
	29. timpani	29._____
	30. bassoon	30._____

Matching: Match each term with its definition:

a. allegro

b. andante

c. arpeggio

d. crescendo

e. homophonic

f. legato

g. monophonic

h. pizzicato

i. polyphonic

j. staccato

31. short, detached style of playing or singing a melody   31._____

32. tempo marking for *fast*   32._____

33. plucking the strings of a string instrument
    instead of using a bow   33._____

34. gradual increase in loudness   34._____

35. sounding the individual tones of a chord one after another,
    instead of together; broken chord   35._____

36. smooth, connected style of playing or singing a melody   36._____

37. texture in which two or more melodies of equal interest are
    performed at the same time   37._____

38. texture in which one main melody predominates over a
    subordinate chordal accompaniment   38._____

39. texture of a single melodic line without accompaniment   39._____

40. tempo marking for moderately slow; a walking pace   40._____

II.
THE MIDDLE AGES AND RENAISSANCE

II-1. MUSIC IN THE MIDDLE AGES (450-1450)

BASIC TERMS:

Gregorian chant	drone	mass ordinary
church modes	organum	

SELF-TEST Multiple-choice: Circle the answer that best completes each item.

1. Gregorian chant
   a. is monophonic in texture
   b. is polyphonic in texture
   c. is homophonic in texture
   d. has no texture

2. The wandering minstrels, or *jongleurs*, of the Middle Ages
   a. performed music and acrobatics in castles, taverns, and town squares
   b. lived on the lowest level of society
   c. played instrumental dances on harps, fiddles, and lutes
   d. all of the above

3. The notation of the secular songs of the Middle Ages does not indicate
   a. rhythm   b. pitch   c. duration   d. any of the above

4. The church modes are
   a. different from the major and minor scales in that they consist of only six different tones
   b. different from the major and minor scales in that they consist of only five different tones
   c. like the major and minor scales in that they consist of seven tones and an eighth tone
      that duplicates the first an octave higher
   d. completely different from any other form of scale

5. The first large body of secular songs that survives in decipherable notation was composed during
   a. the ninth century by monks for church services
   b. the twelfth and thirteenth centuries by French nobles called *troubadours* and *trouvères*
   c. the fourteenth century by Guillaume de Machaut and his contemporaries
   d. the fifteenth century by wandering minstrels called *jongleurs*

6. The *ars nova*, or *new art*, of the fourteenth century differed from older music in that
   a. a new system of notation permitted composers to specify almost any rhythmic pattern
   b. the subjects were all secular
   c. there was no syncopation
   d. the music emphasized homophonic texture

7. The first steps toward the development of polyphony were taken sometime
   between 700 and 900, when
   a. musicians composed new music to accompany dancing
   b. the French nobles began to sing hunting songs together
   c. monks in monastery choirs began to add a second melodic line to Gregorian chant
   d. all of the above

8. The *Notre Dame* Mass by Guillaume de Machaut was
   a. written for three voices without instrumental accompaniment
   b. written for the Cathedral of Notre Dame in Paris
   c. the first polyphonic treatment of the mass ordinary by a known composer
   d. all of the above

9. Leonin and Perotin are notable because they
   a. are the first important composers known by name
   b. indicated definite time values and a clearly defined meter in their music
   c. were the leaders of the school of Notre Dame
   d. all of the above

10. Secular music in the fourteenth century
    a. became more important than sacred music
    b. was not based on Gregorian chant
    c. included drinking songs and pieces in which bird calls, barks of dogs,
       and hunting shouts are imitated
    d. all of the above

11. Gregorian chant is named after Pope Gregory I, who
    a. composed all the chants presently in use
    b. was credited by medieval legend with having created it, even though it evolved
       over many centuries
    c. had his name put on the first printed edition
    d. wrote the texts for the chants

12. The center of polyphonic music in Europe after 1150 was
    a. Paris   b. Rome   c. Reims   d. London

13. Gregorian chant
    a. was the official music of the Roman Catholic church for more than 1,000 years
    b. retained some elements of the Jewish synagogue of the first centuries after Christ
    c. is set to sacred Latin texts
    d. all of the above

14. The French secular songs of the Middle Ages usually dealt with
    a. the Crusades   c. love
    b. spinning   d. all of the above

15. In the recording of the medieval *estampie*, the melody line is played on a rebec, a
    a. medieval drum   c. tubular wind instrument
    b. bowed string instrument   d. plucked string instrument

16. Medieval music that consists of Gregorian chant and one or more additional melodic lines is called
    a. *ars nova*   c. alleluia
    b. organum   d. cantus firmus

17. The foremost composer of fourteenth-century France was
    a. Guillaume de Machaut   c. Charles V
    b. Hildegard of Bingen   d. Perotin

EXERCISE The medieval period:

The term *Middle Ages* implies little more than the period between the "good old days" of Rome, and the "wonderful new days" of the Renaissance. But during this time — a thousand years of human history — something must have happened that would deserve greater distinction. Try to get an overall feeling for the period (actually three distinct periods) by filling in the following chart.

MIDDLE AGES: (450-1450)	DARK AGES (-)	ROMANESQUE (-)	GOTHIC (-)
Personalities			
Events			
Political and economic conditions			
Social life			
Education			
Literature			

The medieval period (cont.)

MIDDLE AGES: (450-1450)	DARK AGES (-)	ROMANESQUE (-)	GOTHIC (-)
Architecture			
Art			
Costume			
Dance			
Vocal music			
Instrumental music			

EXERCISE The church modes:

The church modes were the basic scales of western music during the Middle Ages and the Renaissance and were used in secular as well as sacred music. Originally there were four authentic and four plagal modes, but by the sixteenth century two more of each were added, making a total of twelve modes.

Since these modes are so important to the music of that period, and also to some extent to the music of the twentieth century, you might want to take a closer look at them. For the moment, let us consider only the authentic modes, those whose first step of the scale is also the tonic or *finalis*. Using only the natural notes of the scale (the white keys of the piano), write, and then sing or play, each of the following modes.

THE FOUR AUTHENTIC CHURCH MODES

Dorian
(D-D)

Phrygian
(E-E)

Lydian
(F-F)

Mixolydian
(G-G)

SIXTEENTH-CENTURY ADDITIONS

Aeolian
(A-A)

Ionian
(C-C)

RESEARCH PROJECT   The Mass:

The most solemn service of the Roman Catholic church, the Mass is the ritual celebration of the Eucharist. The liturgy, or public form of worship, is divided into texts that remain the same each day (the *ordinary*) and texts that vary from day to day (the *proper*). Using the framework below, check those sections that were usually set to music. Note particularly their place within the complete ceremony. (If you have the opportunity of hearing a High Mass, see if you can follow the various sections.)

MASS PROPER (changing)	MASS ORDINARY (constant)
_____1. Introit	
	_____2. *Kyrie eleison* (Lord have mercy on us)
	_____3. *Gloria in excelsis Deo* (Glory to God in the highest)
_____4. Collect (Prayer)	
_____5. Epistle [New Testament]	
_____6. Gradual [Psalms]	
_____7. Alleluia (or Tract)	
_____8. Gospel [New Testament]	
	_____9. *Credo in unum Deum* (I believe in one God)
_____10. Offertory	
_____11. Secret	
_____12. Preface	
	_____13. *Sanctus* (Holy, Holy, Holy); *Benedictus qui venit in nomine Domini* (Blessed is he that comes in the name of the Lord)
	_____14. Canon [prayers before and after the Consecration]
	_____15. *Agnus Dei, qui tollis peccata mundi* (Lamb of God, who takest away the sins of the world)
_____16. Communion	
_____17. Post-Communion	
	_____18. *Ite, missa est* (Go, you are sent forth) [congregation dismissed]

II-2. MUSIC IN THE RENAISSANCE (1450-1600)

BASIC TERMS:
word painting   motet   madrigal
a cappella   mass   lute

SELF-TEST Multiple-choice: Circle the answer that best completes each item.

1. The texture of Renaissance music is chiefly
   a. monophonic   b. homophonic   c. polyphonic   d. heterophonic

2. The Renaissance madrigal began around 1520 in
   a. England   b. France   c. Italy   d. Flanders

3. Much of the instrumental music composed during the Renaissance was intended for
   a. the concert hall   c. dancing
   b. religious worship   d. the piano

4. The dominant intellectual movement of the Renaissance was called
   a. feudalism   b. humanism   c. classicism   d. paganism

5. *A cappella* refers to
   a. unaccompanied choral music
   b. men taking their hats off in church
   c. singing in a hushed manner because one is in church
   d. any form of music appropriate for church use

6. The _____ is a stately dance in duple meter similar to the pavane.
   a. galliard   b. passamezzo   c. saltarello   d. minuet

7. Palestrina's career centered in
   a. the Netherlands   b. Florence   c. Naples   d. Rome

8. Renaissance melodies are usually easy to sing because
   a. the level of musicianship in the Renaissance was not very high, and so easy music
      was composed
   b. the music was mostly homophonic, so that one could sing it with a group
   c. there was a sharply defined beat, which kept the performers together
   d. the melody usually moves along a scale with few large leaps

9. Palestrina's *Pope Marcellus* Mass sounds fuller than Josquin's *Ave Maria* because
   a. Palestrina was a better composer
   b. it is set for six voices instead of four
   c. the recording engineer adjusted the levels differently
   d. all of the above

10. Josquin Desprez was a contemporary of
    a. Christopher Columbus   c. Palestrina
    b. Perotin   d. Queen Elizabeth of England

11. The madrigal anthology *The Triumphes of Oriana* was written in honor of
    a. Queen Anne   c. the goddess Diana
    b. King Henry VIII   d. Queen Elizabeth I

12. A madrigal, like a motet, is a vocal composition that combines homophonic and
    polyphonic textures; but it differs from the motet in that it
    a. uses a vernacular rather than Latin text
    b. more often uses word painting and unusual harmonies
    c. both a and b
    d. neither a nor b

13. Thomas Weelkes's *As Vesta Was Descending* is notable for its
    a. word painting   c. instrumental accompaniment
    b. completely homophonic texture   d. monophonic texture

14. The development of the English madrigal can be traced to 1588 and considered a result of
    a. the Spanish armada
    b. a decree by Queen Elizabeth
    c. the writings of Shakespeare
    d. the publication in London of a volume of translated Italian madrigals

Completion: Supply the missing information.

15. The two main forms of sacred Renaissance music are

    the _____ and the _____.

16. The sections of the Renaissance mass are _____, _____,

    _____, _____, and _____.

17. Performing choral music without instrumental accompaniment is

    called _____.

Listen to Josquin's *Ave Maria*, and then complete the following:

18. The work is written for _____ voices.

19. A feeling of continuous flow is created by _____.

20. The opening section, like many later sections, uses polyphonic

    _____, a technique typical of the period.

EXERCISE   People and events in the Renaissance:
 Although some historians place the beginning of the Renaissance as early as 1400, or even earlier, the textbook prefers 1450. Using either 1400 or 1450, list some of the more important personalities and significant events of that period.

PERSONALITIES   EVENTS (include dates)

EXERCISE Differences between the Middle Ages and the Renaissance:
 Referring to the chart you made for the Middle Ages (pages 27-28), explain the differences, if any, between the Middle Ages and the Renaissance in each of the following areas.

Economic conditions:

Social life:

Education:

Literature:

Architecture:

Art:

Costume:

Dance:

Vocal music:

Instrumental music:

LISTENING EXERCISE A comparison of the Medieval and Renaissance styles:
As you listen to three examples provided by your instructor, check those characteristics that are predominant in each composition. When this analysis is completed, decide which style each example represents.

	1.	2.	3.
Melody: angular, rhythmic, narrow range	___	___	___
basically conjunct, greater range, arches	___	___	___
Texture: use of cantus firmus	___	___	___
free polyphony	___	___	___
Rhythm: greater use of syncopation	___	___	___
gently flowing	___	___	___
Harmony: occasional dissonant clashes between parts	___	___	___
basically consonant, triadic	___	___	___
Sonority: two or three voices in upper ranges	___	___	___
full four- to six-voice choirs, with bass range	___	___	___
Language: predominantly Latin	___	___	___
greater use of vernacular	___	___	___

Example 1:

style:

composer: title:

Example 2:

style:

composer: title:

Example 3:

style:

composer: title:

RESEARCH PROJECT Renaissance instruments:

It has been said that the Renaissance had a greater variety of instrumental timbres than we have at present. Classify each of the following Renaissance instruments according to the correct family grouping, and identify the specific characteristics that distinguish it from the other members of the same family.

FAMILY   CHARACTERISTICS

Bagpipe

Cornett

Crumhorn

Curtal

Fiddle

Lute

Mandora

Pipe and tabor

Regal

Sackbut

Serpent

Shawm

Theorbo

Viol

LISTENING EXERCISE Period and modern instruments:

Listen to a Renaissance composition played on modern instruments; then listen to the same composition played on period instruments. Compare the performances with regard to balance, appropriateness of combination, interpretation, and technical execution, indicating similarities and differences. Evaluate the results of each.

Title: Composer:

Modern instruments (performers):
    Comments:

Period instruments (performers):
    Comments:

RESARCH PROJECT Dances of the Renaissance:

Dancing was very popular among all social classes in the Renaissance, and skill in dancing was a very important mark of a gentleman or gentlewoman. Listen to some of the dances popular at that time, and identify the character, purpose (if any), tempo, meter, and basic rhythmic pattern of each.

Allemande:

Basse danse:

Branle:

Canario:

Courante:

Galliard:

Passamezzo:

Pavane:

Saltarello:

Sarabande:

Tourdion:

Volta:

UNIT QUIZ II
THE MIDDLE AGES AND RENAISSANCE

Name_____

Class/section_____Date_____

Matching: Match each term with its definition.

a. a cappella

b. chant

c. church modes

d. jongleurs

e. lute

f. mass ordinary

g. mass proper

h. motet

i. organum

j. passamezzo

k. trouvères

l. viol

m. word painting

1. medieval music consisting of Gregorian chant and one or more additional lines　　1._____

2. wandering minstrels of the Middle Ages　　2._____

3. poet-musicians of the French nobility　　3._____

4. musical representation of specific poetic images　　4._____

5. plucked string instrument with a body shaped like half a pear　　5._____

6. family of bowed string instruments　　6._____

7. unaccompanied choral singing　　7._____

8. scales consisting of seven different tones, whose patterns are different from the major and minor scales　　8._____

9. melody sung without accompaniment　　9._____

10. text portions of the Roman Catholic Mass that remain the same each day　　10._____

11. text portions of the Roman Catholic Mass that change from day to day　　11._____

12. polyphonic choral work set to a sacred Latin text　　12._____

13. stately dance in duple meter　　13._____

Matching: Match each composition with its composer.

a. Josquin Desprez

b. Guillaume de Machaut

c. G. P. da Palestrina

d. Michael Praetorius

e. Thomas Weelkes

14. *Notre Dame* Mass　　14._____

15. *Pope Marcellus* Mass　　15._____

16. *As Vesta Was Descending*　　16._____

17. *Ave Maria . . . virgo serena*　　17._____

18. *Terpsichore*　　18._____

Unit Quiz II (cont.)

Multiple-choice: Choose the answer that best completes each item.

19. The intellectual movement called *humanism*
    a. condemned any remnant of pagan antiquity
    b. focused on human life and its accomplishments
    c. treated the madonna as a childlike earthly creature
    d. focused on the afterlife in heaven and hell   19._____

20. Which of the following is not a part of the Renaissance mass?
    a. Ave Maria   b. Gloria   c. Kyrie   d. Credo   20._____

21. An outstanding composer of the *ars nova* was
    a. Perotin   c. Leonin
    b. Guillaume de Machaut   d. Pope Gregory I   21._____

22. The first large body of secular songs that survives in decipherable notation was composed
    a. during the twelfth and thirteenth centuries   c. from 590 to 604
    b. during the ninth century   d. during the fifteenth century   22._____

23. Which of the following is *not* true of Gregorian chant?
    a. It conveys a calm, otherworldly quality.
    b. Its rhythm is flexible, without meter.
    c. The melodies tend to move stepwise within a narrow range of pitches.
    d. It is usually polyphonic in texture.   23._____

24. One of the major characteristics of *ars nova* music is its use of
    a. syncopation   c. Gregorian chant
    b. organum   d. monophonic texture   24._____

25. An outstanding composer of the Notre Dame school was
    a. Perotin   c. Hildegard of Bingen
    b. Guillaume de Machaut   d. Pope Gregory I   25._____

Listening or essay question: To be provided by your instructor.

_____

_____

_____

_____

_____

III. THE BAROQUE PERIOD

III-1. BAROQUE MUSIC (1600-1750)

BASIC TERMS:

    terraced dynamics   basso continuo (figured bass)
    clavichord   movement

SELF-TEST Completion: Supply the missing information.

1. The medieval church modes gradually gave way to the _____

   and _____ scales in the middle baroque.

2. The two musical giants of the baroque were _____ and _____.

3. A bass part together with numbers (figures) specifying the chords to be played above it,

   characteristic of the baroque, is called _____.

4. The alternation between soft and loud dynamics in baroque music

   is known as _____.

5. A section that sounds fairly complete and independent but is part of a larger composition

   is called a_____.

SELF-TEST Multiple-choice: Circle the answer that best completes each item.

6. One of the most revolutionary periods in music history was the
   a. Renaissance   c. middle baroque
   b. early baroque   d. late baroque

7. The early baroque was characterized by
   a. elaborate counterpoint
   b. homophonic texture
   c. development of the standardized orchestra
   d. diffusion of the style into every corner of Europe

8. The middle baroque was characterized by
   a. elaborate counterpoint
   b. homophonic texture
   c. development of the standardized orchestra
   d. diffusion of the style into every corner of Europe

9. A popular keyboard instrument in which sound was produced
   by means of brass blades striking the strings was the
   a. clavichord   c. organ
   b. harpsichord   d. basso continuo

10. *Affections* in baroque usage refers to
    a. the nobility's manner of deportment   c. terraced dynamics
    b. the doctrine of universal brotherhood   d. emotional states or moods of music

LISTENING EXERCISE A comparison of the Renaissance and early baroque styles:
As you listen to three examples provided by your instructor, check those characteristics that are predominant in each composition. When this analysis is completed, decide which style each example represents:

	1.	2.	3.
Medium: large choral group, a cappella	___	___	___
small vocal ensemble, with basso continuo	___	___	___
Melody: basically conjunct, easy to sing	___	___	___
elaborate, ornamented; difficult to sing	___	___	___
Texture: basically polyphonic	___	___	___
basically homophonic	___	___	___
Rhythm: gently flowing	___	___	___
emphatically rhythmic	___	___	___
Harmony: consonant, triadic, church modes	___	___	___
greater use of dissonances, major and minor tonalities	___	___	___
Dynamics: basically constant	___	___	___
terraced	___	___	___
Timbres: specialized instruments	___	___	___
violin family, familiar instruments, basso continuo	___	___	___

Example 1:

    style:

    composer: title:

Example 2:

    style:

    composer: title:

Example 3:

    style:

    composer: title:

III-2. MUSIC IN BAROQUE SOCIETY

SELF-TEST Multiple-choice: Circle the answer that best completes each item.

1. In the baroque period, the ordinary citizen's opportunities for hearing music usually came from the
   a. court   b. church   c. concert hall   d. corner tavern

2. Frederick the Great, king of Prussia, was a
   a. flutist   c. composer
   b. general   d. all of the above

3. In Italy, music schools were often connected with
   a. orphanages   c. public schools
   b. courts of the nobility   d. universities

4. The music director of a court in the baroque period
   a. supervised and directed the musical performances
   b. composed much of the music required
   c. was responsible for the discipline of the other musicians
   d. all of the above

5. A large court during the baroque period might employ about _____ performers.
   a. 18   b. 24   c. 80   d. 120

III-3. THE CONCERTO GROSSO AND RITORNELLO FORM

BASIC TERMS:

concerto grosso	ritornello form
tutti	ritornello

SELF-TEST Completion: Supply the missing information.

1. A concerto grosso usually has _____ movements.

2. The tempo markings of the movements of a concerto grosso are

   usually _____, _____, and _____.

3. The large group of players in a concerto grosso is known as the _____.

4. The first and last movements of the concerto grosso are often in _____ form.

5. The solo instruments in Bach's *Brandenburg* Concerto No. 5 are the

   _____, _____, and _____.

LISTENING EXERCISE A *Brandenburg* Concerto:
Having studied Bach's *Brandenburg* Concerto No. 5, listen to one of the other five concertos and find similarities and differences. While listening, complete the following.

Johann Sebastian Bach: *BRANDENBURG* CONCERTO No.____

Performers:
____live performance   ____recorded performance

Instrumentation:
concertino (solo group):
ripieno (tutti):

Order of movements:
For each movement, in addition to the tempo, form, and mood requested, give any other characteristics you recognize, such as terraced dynamics, changes in texture, strong rhythmic drive, basso ostinato, improvisation, the realization of a basso continuo, or elaborate ornamentation.

First movement:
tempo: form: mood:

comments:

Second movement:
tempo: form: mood:

comments:

Third movement:
tempo: form: mood:

comments:

Fourth movement:
tempo: form: mood:

comments:

Comparison with the *Brandenburg* Concerto No. 5:
similarities:

differences:

III-4. THE FUGUE

BASIC TERMS:

fugue	pedal point (organ point)
subject	inversion
answer	retrograde
countersubject	augmentation
episode	diminution
stretto	prelude

SELF-TEST Matching: Match each term with its description.

1. answer

2. augmentation

3. countersubject

4. diminution

5. episodes

6. inversion

7. pedal point

8. retrograde

9. stretto

10. subject

a. presentation of a subject from right to left, or beginning with the last note and proceeding backward to the first

b. main theme of a fugue

c. imitation of a subject before it is completed

d. subject of a fugue presented in the dominant

e. presentation of a subject in lengthened time values

f. presentation of a subject in shortened time values

g. melodic idea that constantly accompanies the subject of a fugue

h. turning the subject of a fugue upside down, or reversing the direction of each interval

i. single tone, usually in the bass, that is held while the other voices produce a series of changing harmonies against it

j. transitional sections of a fugue that offer either new material or fragments of the subject or countersubject

LISTENING EXERCISE Bach's Organ Fugue in G Minor:

After listening several times to the subject of Bach's Organ Fugue in G Minor (*Little* Fugue), you should be able to recognize it regardless of accompanying material. Complete the following diagram by sketching in the relative pitch levels of the entrances of the subject (the first two are already indicated). Draw vertical lines to indicate episodes where the subject is not presented in its entirety.

1----------

2----------

RESEARCH PROJECT Transcriptions of Bach's Organ Fugue in G Minor:

Compare the original organ version of Bach's *Little* Fugue with two transcriptions. Which do you prefer from an aesthetic point of view? Why? Which do you prefer for personal listening? Why?

Medium: organ   _____ _____

Performer:

Comments:

Preferences:
(include reasons)

III-5. THE ELEMENTS OF OPERA

BASIC TERMS:

opera
libretto
librettist
voice categories of opera

aria
recitative
ensemble
prompter
overture (prelude)

SELF-TEST Matching: Match each term with its description.

1. aria

2. basso buffo

3. basso profundo

4. conductor

5. duet

6. ensemble

7. libretto

8. opera

9. overture

10. prompter

11. recitative

12. supernumeraries

a. play, set to music and sung to orchestral accompaniment, with scenery, costumes, and action

b. singer with a low range who usually takes comic roles

c. musical number for two solo voices with orchestral accompaniment

d. song for solo voice with orchestral accompaniment

e. singer with a very low range and powerful voice, who usually takes roles calling for great dignity

f. vocal line that imitates the rhythms and pitch fluctuations of speech

g. person who beats time, indicates expression, cues in musicians, and controls the balance among instruments and voices

h. people on the opera stage who do not sing, but carry spears, fill out crowds, drink wine, or do other things that add to the opera's effect

i. text, or book, of a musical dramatic work

j. operatic number in which three or more lead singers are involved

k. orchestral composition performed before the curtain rises on a dramatic work

l. person who gives cues and reminds singers of words or pitches if they momentarily lose their place

RESEARCH PROJECT Preparing for a visit to the opera:

Either on your own or as part of a class project, begin preparing for a visit to the opera. Whether for a live performance, a television broadcast, or a Saturday radio broadcast by the Metropolitan Opera, a little advance preparation can greatly enhance your appreciation and enjoyment of the performance.

Name of the opera:

Composer: Language:

Historical time: Place:

Comic or tragic:

Main characters:

Summary of plot or argument:

High points to look and listen for:

"Hit tunes":

III-6. OPERA IN THE BAROQUE ERA

BASIC TERMS:

Camerata   secco recitative   da capo aria
castrato (castrati)   accompanied recitative   da capo

SELF-TEST Multiple-choice: Circle the answer that best completes each item.

1. Most early baroque operas were based on Greek mythology and
   a. contemporary political events
   b. contemporary lyric poetry
   c. contemporary exploration of the new world
   d. ancient history

2. Members of the Camerata wanted to create a new vocal style based on the
   a. music of the ancient Greek tragedies
   b. glories of their aristocratic patrons
   c. organum of the Middle Ages
   d. polyphonic madrigal

3. A typical baroque operatic form was the da capo aria in ABA form in which the singer
   a. would make a literal repetition of the opening A section after the B section
   b. was expected to embellish the returning melody with ornamental tones
   c. would insert recitatives between the sections for added variety
   d. improvise new words for the returning A section

4. The first opera house in Europe to offer entry to anyone with the price of admission opened in 1637 in
   a. Hamburg   b. London   c. Rome   d. Venice

5. The members of the Camerata wanted the vocal line of their music to follow
   a. standard rules of musical theory   c. the lines of contrapuntal writing
   b. the rhythms and pitch fluctuations of speech d. set metrical and melodic patterns

6. Speechlike melody accompanied only by a basso continuo is called
   a. secco recitative   c. castrato
   b. accompanied recitative   d. basso ostinato

7. Embellishments are
   a. ornamental tones not printed in the music that seventeenth- and
      eighteenth-century performers were expected to add to the melody
   b. music created at the same time it is performed
   c. notes printed in the music that embellish the melody
   d. obsolete in contemporary performances

III-7. CLAUDIO MONTEVERDI

SELF-TEST Multiple-choice: Circle the answer that best completes each item.

1. Monteverdi spent the greater part of his career in the most important church post in Italy, that of
   a. Notre Dame, Paris
   b. The Duomo, Florence
   c. St. Mark's, Venice
   d. the Vatican, Rome

2. To achieve intensity of expression, Monteverdi used _____ with unprecedented freedom and daring.
   a. consonance   b. dissonance   c. basso continuo   d. texts

3. Orpheus goes to Hades in the hope of bringing _____ back to life.
   a. Eurydice   b. Phyllis   c. Persephone   d. Oriana

4. Which of the following statements is *not* true?
   a. Monteverdi's *Orfeo*, written in 1607, is considered to be the earliest operatic masterpiece.
   b. All twelve of Monteverdi's operas are regularly performed in Europe and America.
   c. Monteverdi creates variety in *Orfeo* by using many kinds of music, combining recitatives, arias, duets, choruses, and instrumental interludes into one dramatic whole.
   d. Monteverdi's works form a musical bridge between the sixteenth and seventeenth centuries and greatly influenced composers of the time.

5. To evoke angry or warlike feelings in some of his texts, Monteverdi introduced new orchestral effects, including pizzicato and
   a. tremolo   b. double stops   c. sul ponticello   d. col legno

6. Monteverdi's vocal music was ordinarily supported by a _____ and other instruments.
   a. bassoon   b. trumpet   c. basso continuo   d. string bass

III-8. HENRY PURCELL

BASIC TERM:
   ground bass (basso ostinato)

SELF-TEST Completion: Supply the missing information.

1. A common variation form in the baroque is the ground bass, or _____.

2. *Dido and Aeneas*, which many people consider the finest opera ever written to an English text, was inspired by Virgil's epic poem, the _____; it was written for students at a _____; it has a great number of dances (more so than is usual in opera) because _____; and is scored for _____.

3. Some indication of the acclaim and respect given Purcell by his contemporaries in England can be seen from the fact that he is buried in _____.

III-9. THE BAROQUE SONATA

BASIC TERMS:

sonata   trio sonata   opus

SELF-TEST Multiple-choice: Circle the answer that best completes each item.
1. Baroque trio sonatas usually involve _____ performers.
   a. two   b. three   c. four   d. five

2. The sonata in the baroque period was a composition in several movements for
   a. a solo instrument   c. two to four instruments
   b. three solo instruments   d. one to eight instruments

3. Corelli's Trio Sonata in A Minor, Op. 3, No. 10, is scored for
   a. two violins   c. two violins and basso continuo
   b. solo violin and orchestra   d. piano, violin and cello

4. Characteristic of baroque trio sonatas, the second movement of Corelli's Trio Sonata in A Minor, Op. 3, No. 10, is
   a. slow and dignified   b. songlike   c. fuguelike   d. a dance

5. The abbreviation *op.* stands for *opus*, Latin for
   a. a cartoon character   b. Spring   c. work   d. opulent

III-10. ANTONIO VIVALDI

BASIC TERMS:

solo concerto   trill

SELF-TEST Multiple-choice: Circle the answer that best completes each item.
1. Vivaldi is closely identified with the musical life of
   a. Rome   b. Venice   c. Florence   d. Cremona

2. Vivaldi wrote approximately _____ concertos.
   a. 10   b. 30   c. 95   d. 450

3. Vivaldi wrote concertos
   a. only for string instruments   c. for a great variety of instruments
   b. only for violins with continuo   d. only for keyboard instruments

4. Vivaldi was famous and influential as a virtuoso
   a. harpsichordist   b. opera singer   c. lutenist   d. violinist

5. A Vivaldi concerto usually has _____ movements.
   a. a variable number of   b. two   c. three   d. four

6. A musical ornament consisting of rapid alternation of two tones that are a whole step or half step apart is a _____.
   a. trill   b. shake   c. blurb   d. wobble

III-11. JOHANN SEBASTIAN BACH

BASIC TERM:
improvisation

SELF-TEST Completion: Supply the missing information.

1. The longest period of Bach's professional life was spent as director of music at St. Thomas Church

   in _____.

2. Bach's church music uses operatic forms such as the _____

   and _____.

3. A collection of compositions that displays all the resources of fugue writing is Bach's

   _____.

4. Bach's works are unique in their combination of rich _____

   and _____ texture.

5. A collection of twice twenty-four preludes and fugues, one in each major and minor key, basic to

   the repertory of keyboard players today, is Bach's _____

SELF-TEST Multiple-choice: Circle the answer that best completes each item.

6. Bach achieves unity of mood in his compositions by using
   a. homophonic texture
   b. musical symbolism
   c. an insistent rhythmic drive
   d. simple melodic ideas

7. Of Bach's twenty children, _____ went on to become well-known composers.
   a. two
   b. three
   c. four
   d. five

8. Bach created masterpieces in every baroque form except the
   a. opera
   b. concerto
   c. fugue
   d. sonata

9. Bach's personal music style was drawn from
   a. Italian concertos
   b. French dance pieces
   c. German church music
   d. all of the above

10. Bach was recognized as the most eminent _____ of his day.
    a. organist
    b. composer
    c. violinist
    d. cellist

III-12. THE BAROQUE SUITE

BASIC TERMS:

suite   French overture

SELF-TEST Multiple-choice: Circle the answer that best completes each item.

1. Baroque suites frequently begin with a
   a. French overture   b. gavotte   c. gigue   d. sarabande

2. Although all the movements of a baroque suite are written in the same key, they differ in
   a. meter   b. national origin   c. tempo   d. all of the above

3. Which of the following is *not* a part of the baroque suite?
   a. allemande   b. waltz   c. sarabande   d. gigue

4. The various dances of the baroque suite are usually
   a. polyphonic in texture
   b. in theme and variation form
   c. in AABB form
   d. in ABA form

5. The French overture has
   a. two sections: slow-fast
   b. two sections: fast-slow
   c. three sections: fast-slow-fast
   d. one continuous section

LISTENING EXERCISE Comparing two baroque suites:

Listen to any two baroque suites. See if all the movements are in the same key, indicate any differences from the traditional order of movements, and note the tempo, meter, and character of the individual movements. Distinguish between those movements that are dance-inspired and those that are not.

Traditional order of movements:	FIRST EXAMPLE composer: title:	SECOND EXAMPLE composer: title:

Prelude or introduction

Allemande
(moderate dance from Germany)

Courante
(fast dance from France)

Sarabande
(slow and solemn dance from Spain)

Optional
(gavotte, passepied, loure, air, *etc.*)

Gigue
(fast dance from England and Ireland)

III-13. THE CHORALE AND CHURCH CANTATA

BASIC TERMS:

chorale   chorale prelude   cantata

SELF-TEST Multiple-choice: Circle the answer that best completes each item.

1. The _____ is an instrumental composition based on a chorale.
   a. cantata   c. chorale prelude
   b. solo concerto   d. French overture

2. In Bach's day, the Lutheran church service lasted about _____ hour(s).
   a. one   b. two   c. three   d. four

3. The _____ is a Lutheran congregational hymn tune.
   a. cantata   b. chorale   c. chorale prelude   d. recitative

4. In their use of aria, duet, and recitative, Bach's cantatas closely resembled the _____ of the time.
   a. suites   b. operas   c. concertos   d. sonatas

5. A sung piece, or choral work with or without vocal soloists, usually
   with orchestral accompaniment, is the
   a. cantata   c. concerto grosso
   b. chorale prelude   d. sonata

III-14. THE ORATORIO

BASIC TERM:

oratorio

SELF-TEST Multiple-choice: Circle the answer that best completes each item.

1. Oratorios first appeared in
   a. Germany   b. England   c. Italy   d. France

2. The first oratorios were based on
   a. Greek mythology   c. Greek and Roman literature
   b. contemporary literature   d. stories from the Bible

3. Oratorio differs from opera in that it has no
   a. orchestral accompaniment   c. choral parts
   b. acting, scenery, or costumes   d. vocal soloists

4. In oratorio, the story is carried forward by the
   a. arias   b. chorus   c. narrator's recitatives   d. duets

5. An element of the oratorio that is especially important and serves to comment on or participate
   in the drama is the
   a. narrator   b. chorus   c. orchestra   d. vocal soloist

III-15. GEORGE FRIDERIC HANDEL

SELF-TEST Multiple-choice: Circle the answer that best completes each item.

1. George Frideric Handel was born in 1685, the same year as
   a. Johann Sebastian Bach
   b. Arcangelo Corelli
   c. Claudio Monteverdi
   d. Antonio Vivaldi

2. Although Handel wrote a great deal of instrumental music, the core of his huge output consists of English oratorios and Italian
   a. operas   b. songs   c. chorales   d. madrigals

3. Handel's oratorios are usually based on
   a. the Old Testament
   b. Greek mythology
   c. the New Testament
   d. Roman history

4. In addition to being a composer and opera impresario, Handel was a virtuoso
   a. violinist   b. organist   c. cellist   d. trumpeter

5. Handel's *Messiah* is an example of
   a. an oratorio   b. an opera   c. musical theater   d. a song

6. Handel spent the major portion of his life in
   a. Germany   b. England   c. Italy   d. Ireland

7. Which of the following oratorios is *not* by Handel?
   a. *Messiah*   b. *Elijah*   c. *Israel in Egypt*   d. *Joshua*

8. The focus of a Handel oratorio is usually the
   a. soprano soloist   b. chorus   c. orchestra   d. conductor

RESEARCH PROJECTS Handel oratorios:
List some of the other oratorios by Handel with which you may be familiar.

Handel operas:
List some of the operas of Handel that have been revived, with a brief synopsis of their plots, or list some famous arias from his operas that are still performed.

BIOGRAPHICAL SKETCH A baroque composer: _____

Born (year, place):
Died (year, place):

Personal life:

    family:

    health and physiognomy:

    personality:

Career:

    significant places:

    significant people:

    employers or patrons:

    means of earning a living:

    financial situation:

Music:
    style of composition:

    general characteristics:

Output (List some of the major forms in which the composer worked, including the approximate
    number of compositions if significant. List some of the major compositions in each category, check
    those which you have heard, and circle those which you have studied):

Category: _____ _____ _____

Works:

Category: _____ _____ _____

Works:

UNIT QUIZ III
THE BAROQUE PERIOD

Name_____

Class/section_____ Date_____

Matching: Match each term with its definition:

a. aria

b. basso continuo

c. cantata

d. chorale

e. chorale prelude

f. concerto grosso

g. fugue

h. libretto

i. movement

j. opera

k. oratorio

l. overture

m. pedal point

n. recitative

o. sonata

p. stretto

q. suite

r. trill

1. play, set to music and sung to orchestral accompaniment, with scenery, costumes, and action   1.____

2. set of dance-inspired movements   2.____

3. large-scale composition for chorus, vocal soloists, and orchestra, usually set to a narrative biblical text   3.____

4. text, or book, of a musical dramatic work   4.____

5. orchestral composition performed before the curtain rises on a dramatic work   5.____

6. song for solo voice with orchestral accompaniment   6.____

7. sung piece; choral work with or without vocal soloists; usually with orchestral accompaniment   7.____

8. hymn tune for congregational use   8.____

9. instrumental composition in which a small group of soloists is pitted against a larger group   9.____

10. imitation of a fugue subject before it is completed   10.____

11. instrumental composition based on a chorale   11.____

12. single tone, usually in the bass, that is held while the other voices produce a series of changing harmonies against it   12.____

13. bass part together with numbers (figures) specifying the chords to be played above it   13.____

14. polyphonic composition based on one main theme   14.____

15. section of a musical work that sounds fairly complete and independent, but is part of a larger composition   15.____

16. vocal line that imitates the rhythms and pitch fluctuations of speech   16.____

17. instrumental composition in several movements   17.____

18. ornament consisting of the rapid alternation of two tones that are a whole or half step apart   18.____

Unit Quiz III (Cont.)

Matching: Match each work with its composer:

a. Johann Sebastian Bach   19. Fugue in G Minor (*Little* Fugue)   19._____

b. Arcangelo Corelli   20. *Orfeo*   20._____

c. George Frideric Handel   21. *Brandenburg* Concerto No. 5   21._____

d. Claudio Monteverdi   22. *Wachet auf, ruft uns die Stimme*   22._____

e. Henry Purcell   23. *Messiah*   23._____

f. Antonio Vivaldi   24. *Dido and Aeneas*   24._____

                                        25. *Spring* Concerto, Op. 8, No. 1, from
                                            The Four Seasons   25._____

Listening or essay question: To be provided by your instructor.

_____

_____

_____

_____

_____

_____

_____

_____

_____

_____

_____

IV. THE CLASSICAL PERIOD

IV-1. THE CLASSICAL STYLE (1750-1820)

SELF-TEST Completion: Complete the following comparison of the baroque and classical periods by checking the column of the period with which each description is most closely associated.

	BAROQUE	CLASSICAL
1. Interest in forming a total illusion; theatrical	_____	_____
2. Fills the space with action and movement	_____	_____
3. Emphasis on balance and clarity of structures	_____	_____
4. "Age of enlightenment"	_____	_____
5. Louis XIV as the epitome of his age	_____	_____
6. Impartial in approach; reality rather than illusion	_____	_____
7. Complex mixture of rationalism, sensuality, materialism, and spirituality	_____	_____
8. New approach to science based on the union of mathematics and experiment	_____	_____
9. Attempt to recapture the "noble simplicity and calm grandeur" of ancient Greece and Rome	_____	_____
10. Evolution of the standard orchestra of four sections	_____	_____
11. Free interchange of instrumental parts	_____	_____
12. Emergence of major and minor as basis of tonality	_____	_____
13. End of the basso continuo	_____	_____
14. Faith in the power of reason as the best guide to human conduct	_____	_____
15. "Age of grandeur"	_____	_____
16. Period of Voltaire, Diderot, David, Goya, and Hogarth	_____	_____
17. Exploitation of individual tone colors in orchestration	_____	_____
18. Emotional restraint and "good taste"	_____	_____
19. Basso continuo as the nucleus of the instrumental ensemble	_____	_____
20. Period of Galileo, Newton, Bernini, Rubens, and Rembrandt	_____	_____

LISTENING EXERCISE A comparison of the late baroque and classical styles:

As you listen to three examples provided by your instructor, check those characteristics that are predominant in each composition. When this analysis is completed, decide which style each example represents:

	1.	2.	3.
Mood: unified	___	___	___
variety and contrast	___	___	___
Rhythm: single continuous figure	___	___	___
varied, changing, flexible	___	___	___
Texture: predominantly polyphonic	___	___	___
basically homophonic	___	___	___
Melody: elaborate, ornamented, continuously expanding	___	___	___
balanced, symmetrical	___	___	___
Themes: one main theme	___	___	___
contrasting themes	___	___	___
Improvisation: essential	___	___	___
limited to cadenzas	___	___	___
Dynamics: terraced	___	___	___
gradual changes	___	___	___
Timbres: subordinate to other elements	___	___	___
exploitation of instrumental timbres	___	___	___
Orchestra: based on the violin family with basso continuo	___	___	___
standard orchestra of four families	___	___	___

Other characteristics:

Example 1:
  style:

  composer: title:

Example 2:
  style:

  composer: title:

Example 3:
  style:

  composer: title:

IV-2. COMPOSER, PATRON, AND PUBLIC IN THE CLASSICAL PERIOD

SELF-TEST Multiple-choice: Circle the answer that best completes each item.

1. Joseph Haydn was content to spend most of his life
   a. serving a wealthy aristocratic family
   b. as a church musician and organist
   c. as an independently wealthy composer
   d. as a professional free-lance musician

2. In the classical period, comic operas sometimes
   a. were based on the Old Testament
   b. ridiculed the aristocracy
   c. were in Latin
   d. all of the above

3. Haydn's contract of employment shows that he was considered
   a. a skilled servant
   b. a free-lance musician
   c. a visiting guest composer
   d. an equal by his employer

4. Social mobility during the classical period was
   a. a limited sociological factor
   b. ruthlessly stamped out by the aristocracy
   c. promoted and encouraged by the church
   d. an important factor in the rise of the middle class

5. Vienna in 1800
   a. was the fourth-largest city in Europe
   b. had a population of almost 250,000
   c. was the seat of the Holy Roman Empire
   d. all of the above

6. In Vienna, Haydn and Mozart
   a. avoided each other
   b. became close friends
   c. were jealous of each other
   d. never met

7. In the classical period, serious composition was flavored by
   a. folk and popular music
   b. heroic and mythological plots
   c. elaborately ornamented melodies
   d. all of the above

8. The prospering middle class in the classical period sought aristocratic luxuries such as
   a. theater   b. literature   c. music   d. all of the above

9. The *Concert des Amateurs*, an organization in Paris devoted to presenting public concerts, was conducted in the 1770s by
   a. Johann Christian Bach
   b. the Chevalier de Saint-Georges
   c. Ludwig van Beethoven
   d. Joseph Haydn

10. Haydn and Mozart wrote many outdoor entertainment pieces, which they called
   a. sonatas   b. divertimentos   c. concertos   d. symphonies

IV-3. SONATA FORM

BASIC TERMS:

sonata form	bridge (transition)	motive	coda
exposition	development	recapitulation	

SELF-TEST Completion: Supply the missing information.

1. Sonata form consists of three main sections: _____, _____, and _____.

2. A movement in sonata form may be preceded by a slow _____ that creates a strong feeling of expectancy.

3. A transitional passage that leads to a contrasting section is called a _____.

4. The three main sections of a sonata-form movement are often followed by a concluding section known as the _____.

5. Short musical ideas developed within a composition are called fragments or _____.

6. The "K" number that appears after Mozart's works refers to

_____.

Multiple-choice: Circle the answer that best completes each item.
7. Sonata form should be viewed as
   a. a rigid mold into which musical ideas are poured
   b. another term for the symphony
   c. a set of principles that serve to shape and unify contrasts of theme and key
   d. a set of variations on a theme

8. In the exposition of a sonata-form movement
   a. the closing theme is in the tonic key
   b. a new theme is always presented in the bridge
   c. the second theme is in a new key
   d. a new meter enters with the second theme

9. Sonata form is used frequently as the form for the _____ movement of a multimovement work.
   a. first
   b. slow
   c. final fast
   d. all of the above

10. In the recapitulation of a sonata-form movement
    a. all the principal material is in the tonic key
    b. a new theme is presented in the bridge
    c. the second theme is in a new key
    d. there is no second theme

11. At the end of a classical exposition there usually is a
    a. new tempo indication
    b. new time signature
    c. repeat sign
    d. coda sign

IV-4. THEME AND VARIATIONS

BASIC TERMS:

theme and variations

countermelody

SELF-TEST Multiple-choice: Circle the answer that best completes each item.

1. Theme-and-variations form may be schematically outlined as
   a. AABB   b. AA'A''A'''A''''   c. ABA   d. ABACADA

2. Each successive variation in a theme with variations
   a. retains some elements of the theme   c. is usually in the same key
   b. is usually in a new key   d. presents a new melodic idea

3. The _____ movement of Haydn's *Surprise* Symphony is in theme-and-variations form.
   a. first   b. second   c. third   d. fourth

IV-5. MINUET AND TRIO

BASIC TERMS:

minuet and trio (minuet)   da capo   scherzo   serenade

SELF-TEST Multiple-choice: Circle the answer that best completes each item.

1. The minuet is generally the _____ movement of a classical symphony.
   a. first   b. second   c. third   d. fourth

2. The minuet as a whole may be outlined as
   a. ABA   b. AABB   c. ABC   d. AABBCC

3. In many of Beethoven's works, there is a _____ movement instead of the minuet.
   a. presto   b. scherzo   c. fugato   d. ritornello

4. The minuet first appeared around 1650 as a(n)
   a. instrumental composition for concert performance
   b. prayer in Germany at the end of the Thirty Years' War
   c. dance at the court of Louis XIV of France
   d. country dance in England

5. The character of the minuet is best described as
   a. brisk and lively   c. heavy and ponderous
   b. quiet and relaxed   d. stately and dignified

6. The scherzo differs from the minuet in that it
   a. moves more quickly   c. has a different meter
   b. has a different form   d. all of the above

7. As is typical in classical music, the double bass part in Mozart's *Eine kleine Nachtmusik*
   a. sounds the same as the cello part   c. is a separate and distinct bass part
   b. is frequently left out in performance   d. sounds an octave lower than the cello part

IV-6. RONDO

BASIC TERMS:
  rondo   sonata-rondo

SELF-TEST Multiple-choice: Circle the answer that best completes each item.
  1. Because of its character, the rondo most often serves as a
      a. slow movement   b. first movement   c. set of variations   d. finale

  2. A common rondo pattern is
      a. ABACA   b. ABACBA   c. ABBABC   d. ABCBA

  3. The main theme of the rondo
      a. returns only once in the movement   c. seldom ends the movement
      b. is usually slow and dignified   d. is usually in the tonic key

  4. Another common rondo pattern is
      a. ABCBCD   b. ABACABA   c. ABCBAC   d. ABACDC

  5. The rondo was used
      a. exclusively in the classical period   c. as late as the twentieth century
      b. only as an independent composition   d. only in the classical symphony and quartet

IV-7. THE CLASSICAL SYMPHONY

BASIC TERM:
  symphony

SELF-TEST Multiple-choice: Circle the answer that best completes each item.
  1. *Symphony* may be defined as a(n)
      a. musical composition for orchestra, usually in four movements
      b. sonata for orchestra
      c. extended, ambitious composition exploiting the expanded range of tone color and dynamics
          of the classical orchestra
      d. all of the above

  2. The usual order of movements in a classical symphony is
      a. fast, dance-related, slow, fast   c. fast, slow, fast, slow
      b. fast, slow, dance-related, fast   d. slow, fast, slow, fast

  3. The first movement of a classical symphony is almost always fast, and in _____ form.
      a. sonata   b. rondo   c. minuet   d. ABA

  4. ABA form is typical of the minuet or scherzo movement and is also common in the
      a. finale   b. first movement   c. slow movement   d. all of the above

  5. A symphony is unified partly by the use of the same
      a. key in three of its movements   c. tempo throughout
      b. theme for each of its movements   d. all of the above

LISTENING EXERCISE A classical symphony:
   Either on your own or as part of a class project, prepare for a live or televised performance of a classical symphony. As with opera—indeed with any form of music—a little advance preparation can greatly enhance your appreciation and enjoyment of the performance.

Title:_____

Composer:_____ Date of composition:_____

Instrumentation:_____

First movement: tempo_____ meter_____ key_____

     form_____ mood_____

     themes:

     comments:

Second movement: tempo_____ meter_____ key_____

     form_____ mood_____

     themes:

     comments:

Third movement: tempo_____ meter_____ key_____

     form_____ mood_____

     themes:

     comments:

Fourth movement: tempo_____ meter_____ key_____

     form_____ mood_____

     themes:

     comments:

IV-8. THE CLASSICAL CONCERTO

BASIC TERMS:

concerto   cadenza   fermata

SELF-TEST Multiple-choice: Circle the answer that best completes each item.

1. A classical concerto is a three-movement work for
   a. instrumental soloist and orchestra   c. instrumental soloist and piano
   b. symphonic orchestra   d. vocal soloist and orchestra

2. An unaccompanied showpiece for the concerto's soloist is known as a
   a. fermata   c. concerto's solo
   b. cadenza   d. pause

3. The symphonic movement usually lacking in the concerto is the
   a. sonata-form movement   c. minuet or scherzo
   b. slow movement   d. rondo finale

4. The favored solo instrument in the classical concerto was the
   a. violin   b. cello   c. piano   d. clarinet

5. A pause in the score of a concerto is indicated by a
   a. signal from the soloist   c. signal from the conductor
   b. signal from the concertmaster   d. fermata

6. The first movement of a classical concerto
   a. is in the same form as a classical symphony   c. is usually a long cadenza
   b. has two expositions   d. does not have a development section

IV-9. CLASSICAL CHAMBER MUSIC

BASIC TERMS:
chamber music   string quartet

SELF-TEST Multiple-choice: Circle the answer that best completes each item.
1. Classical chamber music is designed
   a. to display the virtuosity of the players
   b. for the intimate setting of a small room
   c. exclusively for performance by paid professional musicians
   d. to be conducted by experienced orchestral directors

2. The classical string quartet is a musical composition for
   a. violin, viola, cello, and bass
   b. two violins, viola, and cello
   c. violin, guitar, viola, and cello
   d. all of the above

3. The most important form of classical chamber music is the
   a. piano trio
   b. string quintet
   c. string quartet
   d. violin and piano sonata

4. The piano trio is a musical composition for
   a. three pianos
   b. violin and piano
   c. violin, cello, and piano
   d. all of the above

5. The usual order of movements in a classical string quartet is
   a. fast, slow, minuet or scherzo, fast
   b. fast, slow, fast, slow
   c. slow, fast, slow, fast
   d. fast, slow, fast

6. A major factor that distinguishes chamber music from the symphony or concerto is that chamber music
   a. does not use sonata form
   b. is performed in concert in concert halls
   c. does not have difficult parts
   d. is performed by one player per part

IV-10. JOSEPH HAYDN

SELF-TEST Completion: Supply the missing information.

1. Haydn was fortunate in having a long and fruitful, as well as financially stable, relationship with the noble Hungarian family of _____.

2. The twelve symphonies Haydn wrote for the concert manager J. P. Salomon for performance at his public concerts are also known as the _____ symphonies, for the city in which they were first performed.

3. Haydn was a prolific composer, as demonstrated in part by his 68 _____ and 104 _____.

4. Haydn's two popular oratorios are entitled _____ and _____.

SELF-TEST Multiple-choice: Circle the answer that best completes each item.

5. Along with his symphonies, Haydn's _____ are considered his most important works.
   a. operas   b. string quartets   c. baryton trios   d. serenades

6. Haydn's duties while in the service of the Esterházys included
   a. composing all the music requested by his patron
   b. conducting the orchestra of about twenty-five players
   c. coaching the singers for operatic performances
   d. all of the above

7. Which of the following is *not* a characteristic of Haydn's music?
   a. The music is robust and direct, radiating a healthy optimism.
   b. The minuets often romp and stomp rather than bow and curtsy.
   c. There are few changes in texture and orchestration.
   d. Many works have a folk flavor, due to the use of actual peasant tunes and original melodies in folklike style.

LISTENING EXERCISE: Nicknames in Haydn's music:
   Many of Haydn's symphonies and string quartets have nicknames. From your listening experiences, identify some of these compositions, and give the nickname and the factors that caused the association:

Work: Nickname:

   Reason:

Work: Nickname:

   Reason:

Work: Nickname:

   Reason:

BIOGRAPHICAL SKETCH A classical composer: Joseph Haydn *or* Wolfgang Amadeus Mozart

Born (year, place):
Died (year, place):

Personal life:

    family:

    health and physiognomy:

    personality:

Career:

    significant places:

    significant people:

    employers or patrons:

    means of earning a living:

    financial situation:

Music:
    style of composition:

    general characteristics:

Output (List some of the major forms in which the composer worked, including the approximate number of compositions if significant. List some of the major compositions in each category, check those which you have heard, and circle those which you have studied):

Category: _____ _____ _____

Works:

Category: _____ _____ _____

Works:

IV-11. WOLFGANG AMADEUS MOZART

SELF-TEST Multiple-choice: Circle the answer that best completes each item.

1. By the age of six, Mozart could
   a. play the harpsichord and violin
   b. improvise fugues and write minuets
   c. read music perfectly at sight
   d. all of the above

2. Don Giovanni, in Mozart's opera of that name, is
   a. a despotic Italian nobleman
   b. the legendary Spanish lover
   c. Sir John Falstaff
   d. the servant to Leporello

3. Mozart's Requiem was
   a. composed by a nobleman using Mozart's name
   b. a high point in his career
   c. an early work
   d. finished by one of his pupils

4. Mozart's trips to Italy
   a. enabled him to study and master the Italian operatic style
   b. were quite rare
   c. were the scenes of his greatest triumphs
   d. enabled him to secure several permanent posts

5. Between the ages of six and fifteen, Mozart
   a. received an excellent formal education in Salzburg
   b. went to Vienna to study with Haydn
   c. was continually on tour in England and Europe
   d. played in the archbishop's orchestra in Salzburg

6. Mozart's Symphony No. 40
   a. is in G major
   b. has only three movements
   c. is one of his last three symphonies
   d. all of the above

7. Mozart's finest German opera was
   a. *The Magic Flute*
   b. *The Marriage of Figaro*
   c. *Don Giovanni*
   d. *Fidelio*

8. Mozart was born in
   a. Salzburg, Austria   b. Eisenach, Germany   c. Bonn, Germany   d. Rohrau, Austria

9. Which of the following is *not* one of Mozart's three masterpieces of Italian opera?
   a. *The Marriage of Figaro* b. *Cosi fan tutte*   c. *Orfeo*   d. *Don Giovanni*

10. The cadenza in the first movement of Mozart's Piano Concerto No. 23 in A major is unusual in that
   a. it serves as a transition to the recapitulation
   b. the performer is expected to improvise at the performance
   c. it was composed by Mozart himself
   d. it was composed by Beethoven

IV-12. LUDWIG VAN BEETHOVEN

SELF-TEST Completion: Supply the missing information.

1. Beethoven's Ninth Symphony is unusual in that it is scored for _____ and

_____ as well as orchestra.

2. We have a record of Beethoven's struggle with his musical material because of his habit of carrying

_____.

3. Beethoven's only opera is entitled _____.

4. Beethoven's Third Symphony was originally composed to commemorate the deeds of
_____ as the embodiment of heroism and democratic ideals. It is said
that when Beethoven heard what this person had done, he tore up the title page, and the
symphony is now known as the _____.

5. Beethoven, as the musical heir of Haydn and Mozart, bridged the

_____ and _____ periods.

SELF-TEST Multiple-choice: Circle the answer that best completes each item.
6. Beethoven's greatest liturgical music is to be found in his
   a. Mass in B Minor
   b. *Missa Solemnis*
   c. *Fidelio*
   d. Eighth Symphony

7. Beethoven's late works, composed after he was totally deaf, include
   a. piano sonatas
   b. string quartets
   c. the Ninth Symphony
   d. all of the above

8. Beethoven greatly expanded the _____ section of the sonata-form movement and made
   it more dramatic.
   a. introduction
   b. exposition
   c. development
   d. recapitulation

9. The choral finale of Beethoven's Ninth Symphony is based on
   a. Dante's *Inferno*
   b. Shakespeare's *Midsummer Night's Dream*
   c. Schiller's *Ode to Joy*
   d. Shelley's *Ode to the West Wind*

10. Beethoven's sixteen _____ are generally considered among the greatest music ever composed.
    a. piano concertos
    b. string quartets
    c. piano sonatas
    d. symphonies

BIOGRAPHICAL SKETCH:

Ludwig van Beethoven

Born (year, place):
Died (year, place):

Personal life:

    family:

    health and physiognomy:

    personality:

Career:

    significant places:

    significant people:

    employers or patrons:

    means of earning a living:

    financial situation:

Music:
    style of composition:

    general characteristics:

Output (List some of the major forms in which the composer worked, including the approximate number of compositions if significant. List some of the major compositions in each category, check those which you have heard, and circle those which you have studied):

Category: _____ _____ _____

Works:

Category: _____ _____ _____

Works:

Name_____

Class/section_____ Date_____

Multiple-choice: Choose the answer that best completes each sentence:

1. The character of the minuet is best described as
   a. heavy and ponderous
   b. brisk and lively
   c. stately and dignified
   d. quiet and relaxed

   1._____

2. A common rondo pattern is
   a. AABB
   b. ABA
   c. ABCBA
   d. ABACABA

   2._____

3. A brilliant solo section in a concerto designed to display the performer's virtuosity
   is called
   a. a cadenza
   b. a fermata
   c. a pause
   d. da capo

   3._____

4. The usual order of movements in a classical symphony is
   a. fast, slow, fast
   b. slow, fast, slow, fast
   c. fast, slow, dance-related, fast
   d. slow, fast, fast

   4._____

5. The typical orchestra of the classical period consisted of
   a. a loose ensemble of available instruments
   b. strings, pairs of woodwinds, horns, trumpets, and timpani
   c. strings with harpsichord continuo
   d. woodwinds, trombones, drums, and strings

   5._____

6. In many of Beethoven's works there is a _____ movement instead of the minuet.
   a. presto
   b. scherzo
   c. fugato
   d. theme-and-variations

   6._____

7. A symphony is a
   a. sonata for orchestra
   b. work for solo instrument
   c. work for chorus and orchestra
   d. work for piano solo

   7._____

8. The standard catalog of the compositions of Mozart was made by
   a. Ludwig von Köchel
   b. Franz X. Süssmayr
   c. Lorenzo da Ponte
   d. Friedrich Kuhlau

   8._____

9. Chamber music is characterized by
   a. having one performer per part
   b. having each player play very difficult solo passages
   c. a lack of repertoire
   d. being worth playing only in intimate chambers

   9._____

10. A string quartet is a musical composition for
    a. flute, violin, viola, and cello
    b. violin, guitar, viola, and cello
    c. violin, viola, cello, and bass
    d. two violins, viola, and cello

    10._____

Unit Quiz IV (cont.)

11. Classicism, as a stylistic period in music, figured prominently during the years
    a. 1450-1600   c. 1750-1820
    b. 1600-1750   d. 1820-1900   11._____

12. Theme-and-variations form may be schematically outlined as
    a. AABB   c. AA'A''A'''A''''
    b. ABA   d. ABACA   12._____

13. The minuet is generally the _____ movement of a classical symphony.
    a. first   c. third
    b. second   d. fourth   13._____

14. The classical concerto is a large-scale work in three movements for
    a. solo instrument and piano   c. solo instrument
    b. solo instrument and orchestra   d. orchestra   14._____

15. A piano sonata is a musical composition in two or more movements for
    a. piano   c. piano and orchestra
    b. piano, violin, and cello   d. flute and piano   15._____

Completion: Name the basic parts of sonata-allegro form:

16._____

17._____

18._____

19. Optional part before 16:_____

20. Optional part after 18:_____

Matching: Match each composition with its composer:

a. Ludwig van Beethoven

b. Joseph Haydn

c. Wolfgang Amadeus Mozart

21. *Eine kleine Nachtmusik*   21._____

22. Symphony No. 94 in G (*Surprise*)   22._____

23. Symphony No. 40 in G Minor   23._____

24. Sonata in C Minor (*Pathétique*)   24._____

25. *Don Giovanni*   25._____

26. *The Magic Flute*   26._____

27. *The Creation*   27._____

28. Symphony No. 3 in Eb (*Eroica*)   28._____

29. *Fidelio*   29._____

30. *The Marriage of Figaro*   30._____

V. THE ROMANTIC PERIOD

V-1. ROMANTICISM IN MUSIC (1820-1900)

BASIC TERMS:

nationalism	program music	rubato
exoticism	chromatic harmony	thematic transformation

SELF-TEST Completion: Complete the following comparison of the classical and romantic periods by checking the column of the period with which each description is most closely associated:

	CLASSICISM	ROMANTICISM
1. Impartial in approach; reality rather than illusion	_____	_____
2. Aristocratic patronage of the arts	_____	_____
3. Emphasis on balance and clarity of structures	_____	_____
4. Emotional subjectivity; fantasy	_____	_____
5. Interest in the strange and the unknown	_____	_____
6. Wide range of emotional expression	_____	_____
7. Nationalism	_____	_____
8. Traditionalism; adherence to established methods	_____	_____
9. Enthusiasm for the culture of the Middle Ages	_____	_____
10. Exoticism	_____	_____
11. Belief in the supernatural; personification	_____	_____
12. Art and culture of ancient Greece as a basic influence	_____	_____
13. Brilliant colors and dynamic motion	_____	_____
14. Emotional restraint and "good taste"	_____	_____
15. Nature as the mirror of the human heart	_____	_____
16. Frequently autobiographical	_____	_____
17. Period of the industrial revolution	_____	_____
18. Individualism	_____	_____
19. Faith in the power of reason	_____	_____
20. Period of the American and French revolutions	_____	_____

LISTENING EXERCISE   A comparison of the classical and romantic styles:

As you listen to three examples provided by the instructor, check those characteristics that are predominant in each composition. Then, decide which style each example represents:

	1.	2.	3.
Style: traditional	___	___	___
individualistic	___	___	___
Mood: restrained, ordered	___	___	___
flamboyant, unpredictable, melancholy	___	___	___
Content: absolute	___	___	___
programmatic, exotic, nationalistic	___	___	___
Melody: balanced, symmetrical	___	___	___
lyrical, individualized	___	___	___
Timbre: moderate variety	___	___	___
rich and sensuous	___	___	___
Orchestra: mainly strings with paired winds and timpani	___	___	___
large size, full instrumentation	___	___	___
Harmony: predominantly diatonic; relatively mild dissonances	___	___	___
prominent chromaticism; more dissonant	___	___	___
Dynamics: moderate range	___	___	___
wide range, sharp contrasts	___	___	___
Pitch: moderate range	___	___	___
wide range; exploitation of extremes	___	___	___
Tempo: relatively constant	___	___	___
fluctuations; use of rubato	___	___	___
Form: moderate in size	___	___	___
miniatures or monumental	___	___	___

Example 1:

 style:

 composer: title:

Example 2:

 style:

 composer: title:

Example 3:

 style:

 composer: title:

V-2. ROMANTIC COMPOSERS AND THEIR PUBLIC

SELF-TEST Multiple-choice: Circle the answer that best completes each item.

1. The composer whose career was a model for many romantic composers was
   a. Wolfgang Amadeus Mozart
   b. Johann Sebastian Bach
   c. Joseph Haydn
   d. Ludwig van Beethoven

2. A composer who earned his/her living as a violin virtuoso was
   a. Clara Schumann
   b. Niccolò Paganini
   c. Robert Schumann
   d. Frédéric Chopin

3. One of the few composers fortunate enough to be supported by private patrons was
   a. Franz Liszt
   b. Franz Schubert
   c. Hector Berlioz
   d. Peter Ilyich Tchaikovsky

4. Music criticism was a source of income for both Berlioz and
   a. Robert Schumann
   b. Franz Liszt
   c. Niccolò Paganini
   d. Giuseppe Verdi

5. When music conservatories were founded, women
   a. were admitted only as vocalists or pianists
   b. were at first accepted only as students of performance, but by the late 1800s could study musical composition
   c. could study only musical composition, since performance was considered undignified
   d. were not admitted

SELF-TEST Completion: Supply the missing information.

6. Because of the _____ and _____, many aristocrats could no longer afford to maintain private opera houses, orchestras, and "composers in residence."

7. A very important musical part of every middle-class home during the romantic period was the _____.

8. Public concerts had developed during the eighteenth century, but only in the nineteenth century did regular _____ concerts become common.

9. It is interesting to note that an American orchestra, the _____, is one of two orchestras that are the third-oldest in the world.

10. Music conservatories were founded in Europe in the first half of the nineteenth century. In the United States, during the 1860s, conservatories were founded in
    _____, _____, _____, _____, and _____.

V-3. THE ART SONG

BASIC TERMS:

art song   through-composed form
postlude   modified strophic form
strophic form   song cycle

SELF-TEST Completion: Supply the missing information.

1. The word _____ is commonly used for a romantic art song with a German text.

2. When music is repeated for all the stanzas of a song, the form is known as _____.

3. When new music is written for each stanza of a song, the form is known as _____.

4. The German composers of art songs favored, among others, the lyric poetry of

_____ and _____.

5. The mood of a song is often set by a brief _____, and then summed

up at the end by a _____, both performed on the accompanying

instrument, the _____.

V-4. FRANZ SCHUBERT

SELF-TEST Multiple-choice: Circle the answer that best completes each item.
1. Schubert
   a. was widely acknowledged as a composer in his lifetime
   b. was very self-critical, which accounts for his meager output
   c. produced his greatest works after the age of forty
   d. was the first great master of the romantic art song

2. The piano's relentless rhythm in *Erlkönig (The Erlking)* unifies the song's episodes and suggests the
   a. galloping horse   c. calmness of the father
   b. joy of the child   d. approach of death

3. Schubert's songs number more than
   a. 50   b. 100   c. 250   d. 600

4. The Erlking, in Schubert's song of that name, is a romantic personification of
   a. ghosts   b. death   c. nature   d. a galloping horse

5. *The Erlking* is a poem by
   a. Heinrich Heine   c. Johann Wolfgang von Goethe
   b. Schubert himself   d. Robert Schumann

6. The form of *The Erlking* is
   a. strophic   c. through-composed
   b. modified strophic   d. none of the above

V-5. ROBERT SCHUMANN

SELF-TEST Multiple-choice: Circle the answer that best completes each item.

1. Schumann's works are
   a. intensely autobiographical
   b. usually linked with descriptive titles, texts, or programs
   c. essentially lyrical in nature
   d. all of the above

2. Robert Schumann's *Carnaval* is a(n)
   a. etude for piano students
   b. song cycle
   c. composition for orchestra
   d. cycle of piano pieces

3. Clara Wieck was
   a. the daughter of Schumann's piano teacher
   b. a virtuoso pianist
   c. Schumann's wife
   d. all of the above

4. During the first ten years of his creative life, Schumann published only
   a. songs   b. piano pieces   c. symphonies   d. musical criticism

5. As a writer and critic, Schumann
   a. founded and edited the *New Journal of Music*
   b. discovered and made famous some of the leading composers of his day
   c. wrote appreciative reviews of young "radical" composers like Chopin and Berlioz
   d. all of the above

LISTENING EXERCISE Lieder: Explore the fascinating world of lieder by listening to some songs of your own choice by Schubert, Schumann, or both.

1. Composer: Title: Form:

   Plot summary:

   Comments:

2. Composer: Title: Form:

   Plot summary:

   Comments:

3. Composer: Title: Form:

   Plot summary:

   Comments:

V-6. CLARA WIECK SCHUMANN

BASIC TERM:
romance

SELF-TEST Multiple-choice: Circle the answer that best completes each item.
1. Clara Wieck Schumann was
    a. a composer
    b. a concert pianist
    c. the mother of a large family
    d. all of the above

2. *Romanze* (*romance*) in the nineteenth century was often used for a(n)
    a. steamy, sexy novel
    b. short, lyrical piece for piano or solo instrument with piano accompaniment
    c. autobiographical song cycle
    d. descriptive programmatic symphony

3. Clara Schumann frequently performed the works of her husband and her close friend
    a. Hector Berlioz
    b. Richard Wagner
    c. Johann Sebastian Bach
    d. Johannes Brahms

4. Clara Schumann
    a. composed many works for orchestra
    b. stopped composing at the age of thirty-six when her husband died
    c. gave up concertizing when she got married
    d. continued to compose music throughout her life

5. As a composer, Clara Schumann
    a. wrote songs, piano pieces, a piano concerto, and a trio for piano, violin, and cello
    b. wrote only operas
    c. wrote only short lyrical piano pieces
    d. never performed her own music

V-7. FRÉDÉRIC CHOPIN

BASIC TERMS:

nocturne   étude   polonaise

SELF-TEST Multiple-choice: Circle the answer that best completes each item.

1. In the 1830s, Paris was
   a. a center of romanticism
   b. the artistic capital of Europe
   c. the home of Victor Hugo, Honoré de Balzac, and Heinrich Heine
   d. all of the above

2. Chopin was
   a. an extroverted virtuoso
   b. robust and flamboyant
   c. sloppy and careless in dress
   d. shy and reserved

3. Most of Chopin's pieces
   a. are exquisite miniatures
   b. are for a wide range of media
   c. have a limited variety of moods
   d. have literary programs or titles

4. Chopin's *Revolutionary* Étude in C Minor develops the pianist's left hand because
   a. the left hand must play rapid passages throughout
   b. it is played only by the left hand
   c. it takes nearly an hour to perform
   d. the left hand plays the main melody

SELF-TEST Completion: Supply the missing information.

5. A study piece, designed to help a performer master specific technical difficulties,

   is known as a(n) _____.

6. A slow, lyrical, intimate composition for piano, associated with night time,

   is known as a(n) _____.

7. The _____ is a dance in triple meter that originated as a stately processional
   for the Polish nobility.

8. Chopin expressed his love of Poland by composing _____

   and _____.

V-8. FRANZ LISZT

BASIC TERMS:
symphonic poem   tone poem

SELF-TEST Multiple-choice: Circle the answer that best completes each item.
1. Among Liszt's favorite inspirations were the literary works of
   a. Johann Wolfgang von Goethe   c. Heinrich Heine
   b. Carolyne Sayn-Wittgenstein   d. Richard Wagner

2. Liszt typified the romantic movement because he
   a. had a charismatic personality   c. was an innovative composer
   b. was a stupendous performer   d. all of the above

3. Liszt's piano works are characterized by
   a. arpeggios   c. an unprecedented range of dynamics
   b. rapid octaves and daring leaps   d. all of the above

4. In many of his works, Liszt unified contrasting moods by a process known as
   a. motivic repetition   c. sequential restatement
   b. thematic transformation   d. cohesive unification

5. During his teens and twenties, Liszt lived in
   a. Rome   b. Weimar   c. Paris   d. Budapest

6. As a youth, Liszt was influenced by the performances of
   a. Richard Wagner   c. Robert Schumann
   b. Hector Berlioz   d. Niccolò Paganini

7. Liszt created the _____, a one-movement orchestral composition based
   to some extent on a literary or pictorial idea.
   a. concert overture   c. piano concerto
   b. symphonic poem   d. sonata

8. Liszt abandoned his career as a traveling virtuoso to become court conductor at _____,
   where he championed works by contemporary composers.
   a. Rome   b. Weimar   c. Paris   d. Budapest

9. Until the age of thirty-six, Liszt toured Europe as a virtuoso
   a. pianist   c. cellist
   b. conductor   d. all of the above

V-9. FELIX MENDELSSOHN

SELF-TEST Multiple-choice: Circle the answer that best completes each item.

1. The high point of Mendelssohn's career was the triumphant premiere of his oratorio
_____ in England.
   a. *Elijah*
   b. *Hebrides*
   c. A *Midsummer Night's Dream*
   d. *Fingal's Cave*

2. Mendelssohn's Concerto for Violin in E Minor opens with a(n)
   a. orchestral exposition typical in concertos
   b. soloist, who presents the main theme
   c. slow introduction by the orchestra
   d. single bassoon tone

3. The three movements of Mendelssohn's Concerto for Violin
   a. are unified by the process of thematic transformation
   b. are all in the same key
   c. all have separate cadenzas
   d. are played without pause

4. In the first movement of the Concerto for Violin, the cadenza
   a. is left to the performer to improvise
   b. appears at the end of the recapitulation, as is common in classical concertos
   c. appears at the end of the development section as a transition to the recapitulation
   d. is frequently omitted in performance

5. Mendelssohn is known as the man who rekindled an interest in the music of
   a. Giovanni Pierluigi da Palestrina
   b. Johann Sebastian Bach
   c. George Frideric Handel
   d. Franz Schubert

V-10. PROGRAM MUSIC

BASIC TERMS:

program music   program symphony   tone poem
program   concert overture   incidental music
absolute music   symphonic poem

SELF-TEST Matching: Match each composition with the category it represents.

1. *The Sorcerer's Apprentice* (Dukas)

                                            a. absolute music

2. *A Midsummer Night's Dream* (Mendelssohn)

                                            b. concert overture

3. *Symphonie fantastique (Fantastic Symphony)* (Berlioz)

                                            c. incidental music

4. *The Moldau* (Smetana)

                                            d. program symphony

5. *Romeo and Juliet* (Tchaikovsky)

                                            e. symphonic poem

6. Symphony No. 40 in G Minor (Mozart)

7. *Les Préludes* (*The Preludes*) (Liszt)

8. *Overture 1812* (Tchaikovsky)

9. *Hebrides* Overture (Mendelssohn)

10. Concerto for Violin and Orchestra (Mendelssohn)

Multiple-choice: Circle the answer that best completes each item.

11. The work referred to by Beethoven as an "expression of feeling rather than painting," was his
    a. Symphony No. 5   c. *Eroica* Symphony
    b. *Fidelio* Overture   d. Symphony No. 6

12. A _____ is a one-movement orchestral composition based to some extent on a literary or pictorial idea.
    a. mazurka   c. symphonic poem
    b. program symphony   d. nocturne

13. The composer who developed the symphonic poem was
    a. Franz Liszt   c. Franz Schubert
    b. Ludwig van Beethoven   d. Richard Strauss

14. Today's movie scores may be regarded as examples of
    a. pure music   c. folk music
    b. incidental music   d. absolute music

15. Nonprogram music is also known as _____ music.
    a. pure   b. absolute   c. concert   d. symphonic

RESEARCH PROJECT The program symphony:
    A program symphony, as its name implies, is a symphony with a program. Each movement of the symphony usually has a descriptive title, and the music suggests or evokes literary or pictorial ideas.

1. List some examples of program symphonies:

TITLE   COMPOSER

_____   _____

_____   _____

_____   _____

_____   _____

2. Listen to one example of your own choice, and complete the following.

Title: Composer:

First movement: title:
    plot summary:

    tempo: mood: form:

    pictorial techniques:

Second movement: title:
    plot summary:

    tempo: mood: form:

    pictorial techniques:

Third movement: title:
    plot summary:

    tempo: mood: form;

    pictorial techniques:

Fourth movement: title:
    plot summary:

    tempo: mood: form:

    pictorial techniques:

(Add fifth movement if there is one).

RESEARCH PROJECT   The concert overture:

As we have seen, an overture is defined as a musical composition performed before the curtain rises on a dramatic work. In this section, we find that the concert overture is not intended to precede a stage work. Instead of the medley type so popular with dramatic overtures, concert overtures are usually in sonata form. List some examples of concert overtures, as contrasted with overtures intended for dramatic works, from your own background, classroom discussion, or the text.

1. List some examples of concert overtures.

TITLE	COMPOSER
_____	_____
_____	_____
_____	_____
_____	_____

2. Listen to one example of your own choice, determine its form, give a brief summary of the plot, and identify those musical characteristics that evoke or suggest programmatic associations.

Title:

Composer:

Form:

Plot summary:

Sound effects (if any):

Musical techniques that evoke literary or pictorial ideas:

RESEARCH PROJECT The symphonic poem:

A symphonic poem—a one-movement instrumental composition associated with a story, poem, idea, or scene—may take many traditional forms (sonata form, rondo, or theme and variations), as well as irregular forms. It is this flexibility of form that separates the symphonic poem, or tone poem, from the concert overture, which is usually in sonata form.

1. List some examples of symphonic poems.

TITLE	COMPOSER	FORM
_____	_____	_____
_____	_____	_____
_____	_____	_____
_____	_____	_____
_____	_____	_____
_____	_____	_____

2. Listen to one example of your own choice, determine its form, give a brief summary of the plot, and identify those musical characteristics that evoke or suggest programmatic ideas.

Title:

Composer:

Form:

Plot summary:

Sound effects (if any):

Musical techniques that evoke literary or pictorial ideas:

RESEARCH PROJECT Incidental music:

If a play is set to music and sung throughout, we call it an *opera*. Some composers wrote music intended to be performed before and during a play. We call such music *incidental* music, for it is intended to set a mood for certain scenes or highlight a particular action on the stage. Movie scores, for example, are categorized as incidental music.

1. List some examples of incidental music.

TITLE	COMPOSER	PLAY AND PLAYWRIGHT
_____	_____	_____
_____	_____	_____
_____	_____	_____
_____	_____	_____

2. Listen to one example of your own choice, and complete the following.

Title: Composer:

Movement or section:

    mood:

    action on stage:

    means of musical reinforcement of action or mood:

Movement or section:

    mood:

    action on stage:

    means of musical reinforcement of action or mood:

Movement or section:

    mood:

    action on stage:

    means of musical reinforcement of action or mood:

Movement or section:

    mood:

    action on stage:

    means of musical reinforcement of action or mood:

V-11. HECTOR BERLIOZ

BASIC TERM:
idée fixe

SELF-TEST Multiple-choice: Circle the answer that best completes each item.

1. In order to support his family, Berlioz turned to
   a. medicine
   b. musical journalism
   c. teaching
   d. arranging concerts

2. Parisians were startled by Berlioz's *Fantastic Symphony* because of its
   a. sensationally autobiographical program
   b. amazingly novel orchestration
   c. vivid description of the weird and diabolical
   d. all of the above

3. In 1830 the Paris Conservatory awarded Berlioz
   a. a graduate fellowship
   b. a scholarship
   c. a position on the faculty
   d. the Prix de Rome

4. The liturgical melody quoted in the last movement of the *Fantastic Symphony* is the
   a. *Ave Maria*
   b. alleluia
   c. benedictus
   d. *Dies irae*

5. Outside France, Hector Berlioz enjoyed a great career as a(n)
   a. conductor
   b. concert pianist
   c. singer
   d. impresario

6. Berlioz's *Fantastic Symphony* is unified by the recurrence of a theme known as the
   a. germ motive
   b. *thème varié*
   c. *idée fixe*
   d. basic motive

7. The *Fantastic Symphony* reflects Berlioz's
   a. intense nationalism
   b. experiences in Rome
   c. love for the actress Harriet Smithson
   d. interest in composing for small, intimate ensembles

8. The fourth movement of the *Fantastic Symphony* depicts a
   a. march to the scaffold
   b. ball
   c. dream of a witches' sabbath
   d. scene in the country

9. Which of the following was not composed by Berlioz?
   a. *Romeo and Juliet*
   b. *The Damnation of Faust*
   c. *The Sorcerer's Apprentice*
   d. Requiem

10. The second movement of the *Fantastic Symphony* is a _____, the most popular dance of the romantic era.
    a. waltz
    b. minuet
    c. country dance
    d. gavotte

RESEARCH PROJECT The changing orchestra:

The text states "as an orchestrator, Berlioz was extraordinarily imaginative and innovative. At a time when the average orchestra had about sixty players, he often assembled hundreds of musicians to achieve new power, tone colors, and timbres." In order to visualize the growth of the orchestra from the baroque through the romantic periods, compare one representative work from each period. Fill in the instrumentation table (see text references), and then arrange the performers into the proper seating plans.

1. Instrumentation table

INSTRUMENTS	Bach (1721)	Haydn (1791)	Berlioz (1830)
piccolo			
flutes			
oboes			
english horn			
clarinets			
bass clarinet			
bassoons			
horns			
cornets			
trumpets			
trombones			
tubas			
timpani			
snare drum			
bass drum			
cymbals			
gong			
bells			
harps			
1st violins	3-5	3-12	12-16
2d violins	3-5	3-12	12-16
violas	1-3	1-8	10-12
cellos	1-3	1-6	8-10
basses	1-2	1-4	4-6
harpsichord			

2. Baroque orchestra, 10-40 players (see text, III-1)

Johann Sebastian Bach: *Brandenburg* Concerto No. 5 in D Major, 1721 (see text, p. 105)

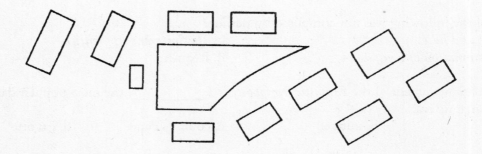

3. Classical orchestra, 20-60 players (see text, IV-1)
   Joseph Haydn: Symphony No. 94 in G Major (*Surprise*), 1791 (see text, p. 164)

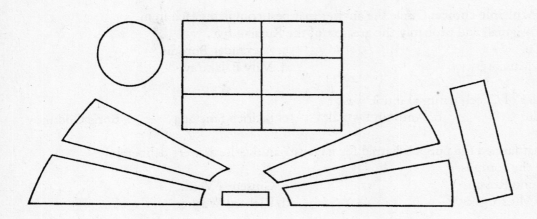

4. Romantic orchestra, approximately 100 players (see text, V-1)
   Hector Berlioz: *Fantastic Symphony*, 1830 (see text, p. 245)

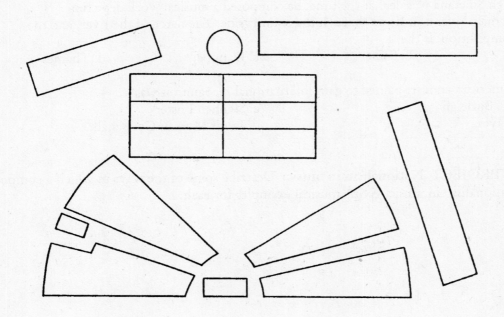

V-12. NATIONALISM IN NINETEENTH-CENTURY MUSIC

BASIC TERM:
nationalism

SELF-TEST Multiple-choice: Circle the answer that best completes each item.

1. The most original, and probably the greatest of the Russian five, was
   a. César Cui
   b. Modest Mussorgsky
   c. Alexander Borodin
   d. Mily Balakirev

2. The founder of Czech national music was
   a. César Cui   b. Antonin Dvořák   c. Bedřich Smetana   d. Boris Godunov

3. Libretti that fanned the public's hatred for its Austrian overlords were deliberately chosen by the composer
   a. Gioacchino Rossini
   b. Modest Mussorgsky
   c. Giuseppe Verdi
   d. Richard Wagner

4. Smetana grew up when Bohemia was under _____ domination.
   a. German   b. Austrian   c. Polish   d. Russian

5. Smetana's most popular opera is _____.
   a. *The Bartered Bride*
   b. *My Country*
   c. *Boris Godunov*
   d. *The Moldau*

6. Even though Smetana was deaf at the time, he composed a musical work depicting Bohemia's main river as it flows through the countryside. The name of the river, and the musical composition, is the
   a. Moldau   b. Seine   c. Danube   d. Thames

7. The first American concert pianist to gain international recognition was
   a. Harry T. Burleigh
   b. Charles Ives
   c. Stephen Foster
   d. Louis Moreau Gottschalk

RESEARCH PROJECT   Nationalism in music: Describe some of the ways in which a composer can express nationalism in music, giving musical examples for each.

RESEARCH PROJECT Nationalistic composers: The text mentions important nationalistic composers of nineteenth-century Poland, Russia, Bohemia, Norway, Finland and America. List some other composers not mentioned in the text whose music has a national flavor.

Culture	Composer	Major Works or Characteristics

V-13. ANTONIN DVOŘÁK

BASIC TERM:
pentatonic scale

SELF-TEST Multiple-choice: Circle the answer that best completes each item.

1. Antonin Dvořák's music was first promoted by
   a. Hector Berlioz
   b. Richard Wagner
   c. Franz Liszt
   d. Johannes Brahms

2. Dvořák _____ quoted actual folk tunes in his compositions.
   a. never   b. rarely   c. occasionally   d. frequently

3. In the first movement of the *New World* Symphony, Dvořák introduces a gracious melody that resembles the spiritual
   a. *Swing Low, Sweet Chariot*
   b. *Nobody Knows the Trouble I've Had*
   c. *Goin' Home*
   d. *Go Down, Moses*

4. In 1892, Dvořák went to _____, where he spent almost three years as director of the National Conservatory of Music.
   a. London   b. New York   c. Prague   d. Leipzig

5. Dvořák "found a secure basis for a new national [American] musical school" in the
   a. music of New York
   b. western art music taught at the National Conservatory of Music
   c. African-American spirituals
   d. traditional folk music of European immigrants

6. The popular character of Dvořák's *New World* Symphony can be traced to the composer's use of _____ often found in folk music.
   a. syncopations
   b. pentatonic scales
   c. modal scales
   d. all of the above

V-14. PETER ILYICH TCHAIKOVSKY

SELF-TEST Multiple-choice: Circle the answer that best completes each item.
1. Nadezhda von Meck was
    a. one of Tchaikovsky's lovers
    b. a wealthy benefactress who provided Tchaikovsky with an annuity
    c. Tchaikovsky's wife
    d. the inspiration for his *Romeo and Juliet*

2. At its premiere in 1870, Tchaikovsky's *Romeo and Juliet* Overture was
    a. a tremendous success
    b. a dismal failure
    c. performed by a large orchestra, with chorus and cannon
    d. enthusiastically applauded by the tsar

3. Which of the following was *not* composed by Tchaikovsky?
    a. Symphony No. 6 (*Pathétique*)   c. *Marche slave*
    b. *Russian Easter* Overture   d. *Overture 1812*

4. Tchaikovsky's *Romeo and Juliet* is a(n)
    a. opera   c. symphonic poem
    b. program symphony   d. concert overture

5. Tchaikovsky's Sixth Symphony
    a. has five movements   c. is in the usual four-movement form
    b. ends with a slow, despairing finale   d. was left unfinished by the composer

RESEARCH PROJECT Tchaikovsky's ballets:
   Tchaikovsky thought of himself as "*Russian* in the fullest sense of the word," yet he is not considered one of the Russian nationalistic composers. This is partly because he fused national and international elements to produce intensely subjective and passionate music. Using his three ballets as examples (as they contain some of his finest music), distinguish the national from the international characteristics of each.

Swan Lake
   plot summary:

   national versus international characteristics:

The Sleeping Beauty
   plot summary:

   national versus international characteristics:

The Nutcracker
   plot summary:

   national versus international characteristics:

V-15. JOHANNES BRAHMS

SELF-TEST Multiple-choice: Circle the answer that best completes each item.
1. Brahms's works, though very personal in style, are rooted in the music of
   a. Joseph Haydn
   b. Wolfgang Amadeus Mozart
   c. Ludwig van Beethoven
   d. all of the above

2. Brahms's musical trademarks included
   a. bombastic flamboyance
   b. the use of two notes against three
   c. the use of da capo arias
   d. all of the above

3. Brahms's masterpiece of romantic choral writing based on texts relating to death
   and resurrection from Luther's German translation of the Bible is
   a. *Four Serious Songs*
   b. *Four Biblical Songs*
   c. *A German Requiem*
   d. Symphony #2 (*Resurrection*)

4. The course of Brahms's artistic and personal life was shaped by the influence of the composer
   a. Antonin Dvořák
   b. Richard Wagner
   c. Franz Liszt
   d. Robert Schumann and his wife Clara

5. In comparison to some earlier composers, Brahms's musical output may be
   considered small. This is explained in part by the fact that Brahms
   a. was too busy conducting and performing to find time to compose
   b. was insecure and lazy, unable to concentrate on composing
   c. was extremely critical of his own work, and endlessly revised his compositions
   d. died before he had a chance to realize himself fully

LISTENING EXERCISE Brahms's music:
   The text states that Brahms "created masterpieces in all the traditional forms" except opera. List your
personal favorites in each of the categories below. (If you don't yet have a favorite in some form, try
listening to some of his music in that form, and see if you don't find one very easily.)

symphony:

chamber music:

piano composition:

song with piano:

song with orchestra:

choral music:

V-16. GIUSEPPE VERDI

SELF-TEST Multiple-choice: Circle the answer that best completes each item.

1. Critics were often scandalized by the subject matter of Verdi's operas because they
   a. symbolized a free and unified Italy
   b. commemorated the Suez canal, which was not even in Europe
   c. were based on Shakespearean plays
   d. seemed to condone rape, suicide, and free love

2. Which of the following operas is *not* by Verdi?
   a. *La Traviata*
   b. *Cavalleria rusticana*
   c. *Il Trovatore*
   d. *Otello*

3. Verdi's great comic masterpiece, written when he was seventy-nine, is
   a. *Il Trovatore*
   b. *Otello*
   c. *Falstaff*
   d. *Aïda*

4. Verdi studied music in _____, the city where Italy's most important opera house, La Scala, is located.
   a. Rome
   b. Florence
   c. Venice
   d. Milan

5. Rigoletto, the title character in Giuseppe Verdi's opera, is
   a. a hunchback
   b. the father of Gilda
   c. a court jester to the duke of Mantua
   d. all of the above

6. Verdi's first great success, an opera with strong political overtones, was
   a. *Oberto*
   b. *Aïda*
   c. *Nabucco*
   d. *La Traviata*

7. Verdi mainly composed his operas
   a. for the Italian musical elite
   b. to glorify the singers
   c. to promote Italian unification
   d. to entertain a mass public

8. The famous aria *La donna è mobile* is taken from Verdi's opera
   a. *Rigoletto*
   b. *Aïda*
   c. *Falstaff*
   d. *Il Trovatore*

9. The soul of a Verdi opera is
   a. extensive thematic development
   b. expressive vocal melody
   c. the situation comedy
   d. atmospheric orchestral parts

10. Verdi's later operas differ from his earlier ones in that they have
    a. less difference between aria and recitative
    b. greater musical continuity
    c. more imaginative orchestrations
    d. all of the above

RESEARCH PROJECT My favorite Verdi or Puccini opera:
     The text mentions some of the operas by Verdi and Puccini that are constantly performed in opera houses throughout the world. Choose your favorite Verdi or Puccini opera, and complete the following (indicate whether you are familiar with the work through recordings or a live performance).

Title:

First performance:

Performance heard or seen (where, when, who):

Characters of the opera, their roles, and voice ranges:

Summary of the plot:

Famous arias:

Romantic characteristics noted:

Why it is my favorite Verdi or Puccini opera:

V-17. GIACOMO PUCCINI

SELF-TEST Multiple-choice: Circle the answer that best completes each item.

1. Puccini's operas have lasting appeal because
   a. he had a marvelous sense of theater
   b. his melodies have short, memorable phrases and are intensely emotional
   c. he minimized the difference between aria and recitative, thus creating a continuous flow of music
   d. all of the above

2. In *La Bohème*, who sings the aria *Che gelida manina (How cold your little hand is!)*?
   a. Mimi   b. Schaunard   c. Rodolfo   d. Marcello

3. Puccini used melodic and rhythmic elements derived from Asian music in his operas
   a. *Turandot* and *Manon Lescaut*   c. *La Bohème* and *Madame Butterfly*
   b. *Madame Butterfly* and *Turandot*   d. *Tosca* and *Turandot*

4. An artistic trend of the 1890s, in which operas dealt with ordinary people and true-to-life situations, was known as
   a. *opera seria*   c. exoticism
   b. *Cavalleria rusticana*   d. *verismo*

5. Which of the following operas was *not* written by Puccini?
   a. *Tosca*   c. *Turandot*
   b. *Madame Butterfly*   d. *I Pagliacci*

6. Puccini's first successful opera was
   a. *Madame Butterfly*   c. *Manon Lescaut*
   b. *La Bohème*   d. *Turandot*

7. *La Bohème* takes place in
   a. Seville   b. Milan   c. Rome   d. Paris

8. Mimi and Rodolfo meet for the first time in *La Bohème* because she has come to his door to ask for a
   a. light for her candle   c. dinner date
   b. drink of wine   d. cup of sugar

9. In *La Bohème*, Rodolfo is a young
   a. painter   c. philosopher
   b. poet   d. musician

10. Which of the following operas is considered an example of *verismo*?
    a. *Turandot*   b. *Tosca*   c. *Nabucco*   d. *Die Walküre*

LISTENING EXERCISE Verismo opera:

Tired of operas dealing with kings, gods, and great heroes, some Italian composers in the 1890s preferred ordinary people and scenes from real life for their subjects. One of the first composers in this movement, known as *verismo*, was Ruggiero Leoncavallo. Since the prologue to his opera *I Pagliacci* can be considered the testament of the *veristi*, it is presented here as an introduction to the discussion of Giacomo Puccini in the textbook.

Ruggiero Leoncavallo: Prologue to *I Pagliacci*

[Tonio, dressed as Taddeo of the Commedia dell'Arte,
puts his head through the curtain, and then advances]

Si può? [salutando] *Signore! Signori! Scusatemi, se da sol mi presento. Io sono il Prologo!*

Permit me? [bowing] Ladies! Gentlemen! Pardon me, if I appear alone: I am the Prologue!

Poichè in iscena ancor le antiche maschere mette l'autore; in parte ei vuol riprendere le vecchie usanze, e a voi di nuovo inviami.

Once again the author brings the old masks before you; partly to remind you of the old custom, he asks me to address you again.

Ma non per dirvi come pria: "Le lacrime che noi versiam son false! Degli spasimi e de'nostri martir non allarmatevi!"

But not to tell you, as before, "The tears we shed are false ones! And don't be alarmed by the sighs we heave, or our sufferings!"

No! L'autore ha cercato invece pingervi uno squarcio di vita. Egli ha per massima sol che l'artista è un uom e che per gli uomini scrivere ei deve. Ed al vero ispiravasi.

No! Your author intends instead to paint you a fragment of life. It is his conviction that the artist is first of all a man, and that he should write for mankind. And the truth has inspired him.

Un nido di memorie in fondo a l'anima cantava un giorno, ed ei con vere lacrime scrisse, e i singhiozzi il tempo gli battevano!

A nest of memories welled up within his innermost soul one day, and the tears accompanied his writing, while his sobs beat the tempo for him!

Dunque, vedrete amar sì come s'amano gli esseri umani; vedrete de l'odio i tristi frutti. Del dolor gli spasimi, urli di rabbia, udrete, e risa ciniche!

So, then, you'll see love as human beings love; you'll see the sad fruits of hatred. The pain of sorrow, howlings of rage, and scornful laughter!

E voi, piuttosto che le nostre povere gabbane d'istrioni, le nostr'anime considerate, poichè siam uomini di carne e d'ossa, e che di quest'orfano mondo al pari di voi spiriamo l'aere!

And you, rather than think of our poor clown costumes, think of our souls, for we are men of flesh and bone, and we breathe the same air in this orphaned world as you!

Il concetto vi dissi . . . Or ascoltate com'egli è svolto. [gridando verso la scena] *Andiam. Incominciate!*

I've given you the idea. . . . Now watch the plot unfold before you. [calling toward the stage] Come on! Let's begin!

[He returns behind the curtain, and it rises]

V-18. RICHARD WAGNER

BASIC TERM:
leitmotif

SELF-TEST Multiple-choice: Circle the answer that best completes each item.
1. The composer who had an overwhelming influence on the young Wagner was
   a. Johann Sebastian Bach
   b. Ludwig van Beethoven
   c. Johannes Brahms
   d. Hector Berlioz

2. Wagner called his works *music dramas* rather than operas because
   a. there is a continuous musical flow within each act
   b. there are no breaks where applause can interrupt
   c. the vocal line is inspired by the rhythms and pitches of the German text
   d. all of the above

3. Wagner's last opera was
   a. *Götterdämmerung (The Twilight of the Gods)*
   b. *Tannhäuser*
   c. *Rienzi*
   d. *Parsifal*

4. The librettos to *The Ring of the Nibelung* were written by
   a. Arrigo Boito
   b. Wagner himself
   c. King Ludwig of Bavaria
   d. Hans von Bülow

5. A short musical idea associated with a person, object, or thought, used by Wagner in his operas, is called
   a. leitmotif   b. lied   c. unending melody   d. speech-song

6. Valhalla, in Wagner's *Ring* cycle, is
   a. a city in New York State
   b. the castle of the gods
   c. the home of Siegfried
   d. the magic ring

7. Wagner had an opera house built to his own specifications in
   a. Munich   b. Weimar   c. Dresden   d. Bayreuth

8. Wagner's first successful opera was
   a. *Tannhäuser*
   b. *Rienzi*
   c. *The Twilight of the Gods*
   d. *Die Walküre*

9. Siegmund, in Wagner's opera *Die Walküre*, is
   a. Sieglinde's brother, then wife
   b. Wotan's son by a mortal woman
   c. Siegfried's father
   d. all of the above

10. Which of the following operas was *not* composed by Wagner?
   a. *Tannhäuser*   b. *Tristan and Isolde*   c. *Fidelio*   d. *Parsifal*

RESEARCH PROJECT Richard Wagner, *The Ring of the Nibelung***:**
Wagner's complete *Ring* cycle was first performed at Bayreuth in 1876. Supply the following for its four operas.

Main characters:

1. *Das Rheingold (The Rhine Gold)*
   plot summary:

   excerpts:

2. *Die Walküre (The Valkyrie)*
   plot summary:

   excerpts:

3. *Siegfried*
   plot summary:

   excerpts:

4. *Götterdämmerung (The Twilight of the Gods)*
   plot summary:

   excerpts:

BIOGRAPHICAL SKETCH A romantic composer: _____

Born (year, place):
Died (year, place):

Personal life:
  family:

  health and physiognomy:

  personality:

Career:
  significant places:

  significant people:

  employers or patrons:

  means of making a living:

  financial situation:

Music:
  style of composition:

  general characteristics:

Output (List some of the major forms in which the composer worked, including the approximate
  number of compositions if significant. List some of the major compositions in each category, check
  those which you have heard, and circle those which you have studied):

Category: _____ _____ _____

Works:

Category: _____ _____ _____

Works:

UNIT QUIZ V
THE ROMANTIC PERIOD

Name_____

Class/section_____Date_____

Matching: Match each composition with its composer:

a. Hector Berlioz
b. Johannes Brahms
c. Frédéric Chopin
d. Antonin Dvořák
e. Franz Liszt
f. Felix Mendelssohn
g. Giacomo Puccini
h. Franz Schubert
i. Clara Schumann
j. Robert Schumann
k. Bedřich Smetana
l. Peter Ilyich Tchaikovsky
m. Giuseppe Verdi
n. Richard Wagner

1. *Fantastic Symphony*   1._____
2. *Rigoletto*   2._____
3. *Madame Butterfly*   3._____
4. *Swan Lake*   4._____
5. *La Bohème*   5._____
6. *The Ring of the Nibelung*   6._____
7. *The Erlking*   7._____
8. *Romeo and Juliet* Overture   8._____
9. *Romeo and Juliet* Symphony   9._____
10. *Carnaval (Carnival)*   10._____
11. *The Moldau*   11._____
12. *A German Requiem*   12._____
13. *The Sleeping Beauty*   13._____
14. Romance in G Minor for Violin and Piano   14._____
15. Symphony No. 9 (*From the New World*)   15._____
16. *Transcendental Étude* No. 10   16._____
17. *Die Walküre*   17._____
18. Étude in C Minor *(Revolutionary)*   18._____
19. *A Midsummer Night's Dream*   19._____
20. *The Nutcracker*   20._____

Multiple-choice: Choose the answer that best completes each item.

21. Instrumental music endowed with literary or pictorial associations, popular during the romantic period, is called
    a. absolute music   c. program music
    b. opera   d. symphony   21._____

22. The deliberate intent to draw creative inspiration from the composer's own homeland is known as
    a. exoticism   c. *verismo*
    b. nationalism   d. individualism   22._____

23. The typical orchestra of the late romantic period numbered about _____ musicians.
    a. 15   b. 24   c. 40   d. 100   23._____

24. Music intended to be performed before or during a play, to set the mood for scenes or highlight dramatic action, is known as
    a. play music   c. absolute music
    b. incidental music   d. music drama   24._____

25. Instrumental music which is written for its own sake, and for which the composer does not provide a program, is called
    a. absolute music   c. music for its own sake
    b. program music   d. opera   25._____

Unit Quiz V (cont.)

26. Drawing creative inspiration from cultures of lands foreign to the composer is known as
    a. exoticism   b. nationalism   c. program music   d. *verismo*   26._____

27. Approximately, the romantic period encompassed the years
    a. 1450-1600   b. 1600-1750   c. 1750-1820   d. 1820-1900   27._____

28. All the following composers are associated with the romantic period *except*
    a. Giuseppe Verdi   c. Robert Schumann
    b. Wolfgang Amadeus Mozart   d. Frédéric Chopin   28._____

29. Which of the following is *not* a characteristic of romanticism?
    a. nationalism   c. individualism
    b. emotional restraint   d. supernaturalism   29._____

30. The movement in opera known as *verismo* is best exemplified by
    a. Claudio Monteverdi   c. Giacomo Puccini
    b. Wolfgang Amadeus Mozart   d. Richard Wagner   30._____

Matching: Match each term with its definition:

a. étude   31. song form in which new music is written for each stanza   31._____

b. leitmotif   32. study piece, designed to help a performer master specific technical difficulties   32._____

c. lied

d. nocturne   33. song form in which the music is repeated for each stanza   33._____

e. polonaise   34. short musical idea associated with a person, object, or thought, used by Wagner   34._____

f. program symphony

               35. romantic art song with a German text   35._____

g. rubato

               36. slow, intimate composition for piano, associated with night time   36._____

h. strophic

i. symphonic poem   37. instrumental composition in several movements based to some extent on a literary or pictorial idea   37._____

j. through-composed

               38. dance in triple meter that originated as a stately procession for the Polish nobility   38._____

               39. one-movement orchestral composition based to some extent on a literary or pictorial idea   39._____

               40. slight holding back or pressing forward of tempo   40._____

VI. THE TWENTIETH CENTURY

VI-1. MUSICAL STYLES: 1900-1945

BASIC TERMS:

glissando	tone cluster	bitonality	polyrhythm
polychord	polytonality	atonality	ostinato
fourth chord			

SELF-TEST Multiple-choice: Circle the answer that best completes each item.

1. Composers in the twentieth century drew inspiration from
   a. folk and popular music from all cultures
   b. European art music from the Middle Ages through the nineteenth century
   c. the music of Asia and Africa
   d. all of the above

2. The combination of two traditional chords sounding together is known as
   a. polytonality   b. bitonality   c. a tone cluster   d. a polychord

3. Among the unusual playing techniques that are widely used during the twentieth century is the _____, a rapid slide up or down a scale.
   a. buzz   b. glissando   c. slip   d. ostinato

4. Which of the following composers was *not* stimulated by the folklore of his native land?
   a. Igor Stravinsky   b. Anton Webern   c. Béla Bartók   d. Charles Ives

5. A chord made of tones only a half step or a whole step apart is known as
   a. polytonality   b. a polychord   c. bitonality   d. a tone cluster

6. The absence of key or tonality in a musical composition is known as
   a. polytonality   b. ostinato   c. a tone cluster   d. atonality

7. To create fresh sounds, twentieth-century composers used
   a. scales borrowed from nonwestern cultures   c. ancient church modes
   b. scales they themselves invented   d. all of the above

8. The use of two or more keys at one time is known as
   a. polytonality   c. atonality
   b. a tone cluster   d. the twelve-tone system

9. A motive or phrase that is repeated persistently at the same pitch throughout a section is called
   a. polytonality   b. glissando   c. ostinato   d. atonality

10. In twentieth-century music
    a. string players are sometimes called on to use the wood instead of the hair on their bows
    b. percussion instruments have become very prominent and numerous
    c. dissonance has been emancipated
    d. all of the above

EXERCISE The twentieth-century context:

The cry is sometimes raised that contemporary audiences listen to music with nineteenth-century ears. Perhaps there is some justification in that complaint, for the twentieth century has seen radical changes in music and it is difficult for the general public to prevent a musical generation gap from developing. Of course, adjustments seem to have been made in other areas: unless the energy crisis takes an extreme turn, for example, no one seriously advocates a return to the horse and buggy. Yet there are people who still refuse to fly.

To place the changes in music in context with similar changes in the other humanities and the sciences, consider life at the turn of the century, at the midpoint, and today. List some of the major stages of development, trends, "isms," and characteristics of each of the following:

	around 1900	around 1945	today
Scientific technology			
Transportation			
Philosophy			
Literature			
Art			
Architecture			
Drama			
Photography			
Motion pictures			
Costume			
Dance			
Sound recordings			

LISTENING EXERCISE A comparison of twentieth-century styles:
    While listening to three compositions in class, or to three works of your own choosing at home, identify the style of each by checking those characteristics that are dominant in each composition. The upper description is usually associated with music before 1900, while the lower is typical of the twentieth century.

	1.	2.	3.
Melody: easy to sing and remember	___	___	___
difficult to sing; asymmetrical	___	___	___
Timbre: rich and sensuous	___	___	___
less emphasis on blended sound	___	___	___
traditional percussion instruments	___	___	___
greater use of percussion and nonmusical sounds	___	___	___
Meter: unified	___	___	___
changing	___	___	___
conventional	___	___	___
unconventional	___	___	___
Rhythm: unified	___	___	___
polyrhythmic	___	___	___
regular	___	___	___
irregular	___	___	___
no jazz elements	___	___	___
jazz elements	___	___	___
Harmony: tonal	___	___	___
polytonal or atonal	___	___	___
predominantly consonant	___	___	___
predominantly dissonant	___	___	___
Ensembles: traditional	___	___	___
unusual	___	___	___
Performance techniques: traditional	___	___	___
unusual	___	___	___
Piano: mainly as a solo instrument	___	___	___
part of percussion section	___	___	___

	TITLE	COMPOSER	STYLE
Selection 1:			
Selection 2:			
Selection 3:			

VI-2. MUSIC AND MUSICIANS IN SOCIETY

SELF-TEST Completion: Supply the missing information.

1. Radio broadcasts of live and recorded music began to reach large audiences during the
   a. 1900s   b. 1920s   c. 1940s   d. 1960s

2. The first opera created for television was Gian-Carlo Menotti's
   a. *Turandot*   c. *Trouble in Tahiti*
   b. *Amahl and the Night Visitors* d. *The Telephone*

3. Recordings of much lesser-known music multiplied in 1948 through
   a. the appearance of long-playing disks   c. government grants
   b. audience insistence for new works   d. demand created by radio stations

4. The most influential organization sponsoring new music after World War I was
   a. the New York Philharmonic Orchestra
   b. the National Broadcasting Company and its orchestra
   c. the International Society for Contemporary Music
   d. the United Federation of Musicians

5. The best-known American ensemble created in the 1930s by a radio network to broadcast
   live music was the
   a. NBC Symphony Orchestra   c. New York Philharmonic Orchestra
   b. Lawrence Welk Orchestra   d. CBS Symphony Orchestra

6. One of the most important teachers of musical composition in the twentieth century was
   a. Amy Beach   b. Nadia Boulanger   c. Sergei Diaghilev   d. Igor Stravinsky

7. Which of the following statements is *not* true?
   a. New technological advances, such as phonograph records, tape recordings,
      radio, and television, have brought music to a larger audience than ever before,
      besides vastly increasing the amount and scope of music available.
   b. Audiences in the first half of the twentieth century, as in Mozart's time, demanded
      and got the latest music, and concert programs consisted mainly of recent works.
   c. Nazi persecution and the onset of World War II led many composers, including
      Stravinsky, Bartók, Schoenberg, and Hindemith, to emigrate to the United States,
      where they made enormous contributions to American musical culture.
   d. American colleges and universities have played a vital role in our musical culture,
      as they have trained and employed many of our leading composers, performers, and
      scholars, have expanded the horizons and interests of countless students, and have
      sponsored performing groups specializing in twentieth-century music.

VI-3. IMPRESSIONISM AND SYMBOLISM

SELF-TEST Completion: Supply the missing information.

1. Impressionist painters were primarily concerned with the

    effects of _____,_____ and

    _____.

2. The most important impressionist composer was

    _____.

3. The term *impressionist* derived from a critic's derogatory reaction to Monet's painting

    _____, exhibited in 1874.

4. Symbolist writers emphasized the purely _____

    or _____ effects of words.

5. Many songs by Debussy use texts by the symbolist poet _____.

SELF-TEST Multiple-choice: Circle the answer that best completes each item.

6. Impressionism as a movement originated in
    a. France
    b. Italy
    c. Germany
    d. England

7. Which of the following is not considered a symbolist poet?
    a. Stéphane Mallarmé
    b. Paul Verlaine
    c. Victor Hugo
    d. Arthur Rimbaud

8. When viewed closely, impressionist paintings are made up of
    a. fine lines
    b. large bands of color
    c. tiny black dots
    d. tiny colored patches

9. The impressionist painters were particularly obsessed with portraying
    a. water
    b. religious scenes
    c. scenes of ancient glories
    d. battle scenes

10. Debussy's most famous orchestral work was inspired by a poem by
    a. Stéphane Mallarmé
    b. Paul Verlaine
    c. Jean-Paul Sartre
    d. Arthur Rimbaud

VI-4. CLAUDE DEBUSSY

BASIC TERMS:

impressionism   pentatonic scale   whole-tone scale

SELF-TEST Multiple-choice: Circle the answer that best completes each item.

1. Debussy's music tends to
   a. sound free and almost improvisational   c. have a strong rhythmic pulse
   b. affirm the key very noticeably   d. use the full orchestra for massive effects

2. The faun evoked in Debussy's famous composition is a
   a. baby deer   c. beautiful young maiden
   b. creature who is half man, half goat   d. sensitive musician

3. As a result of his summer sojourns away from France during his teens, Debussy developed
   a lifelong interest in the music of
   a. Italy   b. Hungary   c. England   d. Russia

4. Debussy's opera *Pelléas et Mélisande* is an almost word-for-word setting of the symbolist play by
   a. Paul Verlaine   c. Maurice Maeterlinck
   b. Arthur Rimbaud   d. Stéphane Mallarmé

5. At the Paris International Exhibition of 1889 Debussy was strongly influenced by the
   a. advantages of modern technology   c. Eiffel Tower
   b. performances of the music of J. S. Bach   d. performances of Asian music

6. In which of the following areas did Debussy *not* create masterpieces?
   a. symphonies   c. chamber music
   b. art songs   d. piano music

7. The poem which inspired the *Prelude to "The Afternoon of a Faun"* was written by
   a. Paul Verlaine   c. Maurice Maeterlinck
   b. Arthur Rimbaud   d. Stéphane Mallarmé

8. In order to "drown the sense of tonality," Debussy
   a. turned to the medieval church modes
   b. borrowed pentatonic scales from Javanese music
   c. developed the whole-tone scale
   d. all of the above

9. Which of the following is *not* characteristic of impressionist music?
   a. a stress on tone color   c. clearly defined rhythmical patterns
   b. a stress on atmosphere   d. fluidity

VI-5. NEOCLASSICISM

BASIC TERM:
neoclassicism

SELF-TEST Multiple-choice: Circle the answer that best completes each item.

1. Favoring clear polyphonic textures, neoclassical composers wrote
   a. fugues
   b. baroque dance suites
   c. concerti grossi
   d. all of the above

2. Neoclassical compositions are characterized by
   a. forms and stylistic features of earlier periods
   b. whole-tone scales
   c. harsh dissonances
   d. use of the twelve-tone system

3. Neoclassicism was a reaction against
   a. romanticism and impressionism
   b. humanism
   c. classicism
   d. traditional forms

4. Which of the following is *not* characteristic of neoclassicism?
   a. emotional restraint   b. clarity   c. misty atmosphere   d. balance

5. Neoclassical composers favored
   a. tonality   b. atonality   c. program music   d. large orchestras

6. A painter who went through a neoclassical phase, and who designed sets for Stravinsky's first neoclassical work, was
   a. Claude Monet   b. Pablo Picasso   c. Auguste Renoir   d. Wassily Kandinsky

RESEARCH PROJECT The music of Igor Stravinsky:

The music of Stravinsky's long and productive life has been divided into three general periods. The text mentions a number of his major works, but by no means all. In a spirit of discovery, listen to at least one work from each period (other than those discussed in the text, if possible), and then compare them to the musical elements discussed in the text. Can you hear differences in each period, and yet enough similarities to cause one expert to write they are all a "continuous evolution toward greater purity of style and abstraction of thought"?

	RUSSIAN PERIOD (1909-1918)	NEOCLASSICAL PERIOD (1918-1951)	SERIAL PERIOD (1951-1971)
Title:			
Comparisons:			
Rhythm:			
Melody:			
Form:			
Timbre:			
Harmony:			
Inspiration:			
Comments:			

VI-6. IGOR STRAVINSKY

BASIC TERM:
primitivism

SELF-TEST Multiple-choice: Circle the answer that best completes each item.
1. During the period from about 1920 to 1951, Stravinsky drew inspiration largely from
   a. eighteenth-century music
   b. Webern's serial technique
   c. Russian folklore
   d. African sculpture

2. *Le Sacre du printemps (The Rite of Spring)* is an example of
   a. neoclassicism
   b. primitivism
   c. serialism
   d. romanticism

3. Sergei Diaghilev was the director of the
   a. Moscow Conservatory
   b. Leningrad Philharmonic
   c. Russian Ballet
   d. Orchestre de Paris

4. Stravinsky's *Rite of Spring* is scored for
   a. a small chamber group
   b. vocal soloists and orchestra
   c. an enormous orchestra
   d. a wind ensemble

5. Which of the following ballets is not from Stravinsky's Russian period?
   a. *The Rite of Spring*
   b. *The Firebird*
   c. *Pulcinella*
   d. *Petrushka*

6. Stravinsky's composition teacher was
   a. Sergei Diaghilev
   b. Modest Mussorgsky
   c. Nikolai Rimsky-Korsakov
   d. Claude Debussy

7. Stravinsky's second phase is generally known as
   a. neoclassical   b. primitive   c. serial   d. postromantic

8. In the 1950s Stravinsky dramatically changed his style, this time drawing inspiration from
   a. Claude Debussy
   b. Richard Wagner
   c. Anton Webern
   d. Russian folk music

9. The famous riot in 1913 was caused by the first performance of Stravinsky's ballet
   a. *Pulcinella*
   b. *The Fairy's Kiss*
   c. *Agon*
   d. *The Rite of Spring*

10. Stravinsky's enormous influence on twentieth-century music is due to his innovations in
    a. rhythm
    b. harmony
    c. tone color
    d. all of the above

VI-7. EXPRESSIONISM

BASIC TERM:
expressionism

SELF-TEST Multiple-choice: Circle the answer that best completes each item.

1. Expressionism is an art concerned with
   a. depicting the beauties of nature
   b. emotional restraint, clarity, and balance
   c. social protest
   d. all of the above

2. The expressionist movement flourished in the years
   a. 1890-1914
   b. 1905-1925
   c. 1914-1941
   d. 1920-1950

3. The expressionist movement was largely centered in
   a. France
   b. Great Britain
   c. Germany and Austria
   d. Russia

4. Twentieth-century musical expressionism grew out of the emotional turbulence in the works of late romantics such as
   a. Richard Wagner
   b. Richard Strauss
   c. Gustav Mahler
   d. all of the above

5. Expressionist music stresses
   a. harsh dissonance
   b. fragmentation
   c. unusual instrumental effects
   d. all of the above

6. Edvard Munch was an expressionist
   a. poet
   b. painter
   c. musician
   d. playwright

7. The expressionists rejected
   a. conventional prettiness
   b. reality
   c. imagination
   d. morality

8. Expressionism stressed
   a. subtle feeling
   b. intense, subjective emotion
   c. reticence
   d. surface beauty

9. Expressionist painters, writers, and composers used _____ to assault and shock their audience.
   a. pastel colors
   b. deliberate distortions
   c. clearly defined forms
   d. vague nature scenes

10. Expressionist composers
    a. contributed many patriotic songs to the war effort
    b. avoided tonality and traditional chord progressions
    c. tried to capture atmosphere with rich, sensuous harmonies and pleasant subjects
    d. all of the above

VI-8. ARNOLD SCHOENBERG

BASIC TERMS:

atonality	twelve-tone system	*Sprechstimme*	tone row (set, series)

SELF-TEST Multiple-choice: Circle the answer that best completes each item.

1. Schoenberg's teacher was
   a. Johannes Brahms
   b. Richard Wagner
   c. Nikolai Rimsky-Korsakov
   d. Schoenberg himself

2. Alban Berg and Anton Webern were Schoenberg's
   a. teachers   b. students   c. predecessors   d. jealous rivals

3. In addition to being a composer, Schoenberg showed skill as a
   a. chemist   b. painter   c. music critic   d. economist

4. Schoenberg developed an unusual style of vocal performance, halfway between speaking and singing, called
   a. *Klangfarbenmelodie*   b. *Sprechstimme*   c. atonality   d. serialism

5. Which of the following statements is *not* true of Schoenberg's twelve-tone compositional method?
   a. The tones of a row may be presented at the same time to form chords.
   b. Each tone of a row must be placed in the same register.
   c. The tones of a row may be placed one after another to form a melody.
   d. A tone row may be shifted to any pitch level.

6. When Schoenberg arrived in the United States after the Nazis seized power in Germany, he obtained a teaching position at
   a. Harvard   b. Yale   c. UCLA   d. Columbia

RESEARCH PROJECT The music of Arnold Schoenberg:

Schoenberg's music, like Stravinsky's, has been divided into three general periods. The text mentions a number of his major works, and discusses examples from the last two periods. Listen to one composition from each period, and then compare the three works with regard to the musical elements discussed in the text.

	POSTROMANTIC PERIOD (1896-1908)	ATONAL PERIOD (1908-1915)	TWELVE-TONE PERIOD (1921-1951)
Title:			
Date:			
Comparisons:			
Rhythm:			
Melody:			
Form:			
Tone colors:			
Dynamics:			
Harmony:			
Tonality:			
Inspiration:			
Comments:			

VI-9. ALBAN BERG

SELF-TEST Multiple-choice: Circle the answer that best completes each item.
1. Georg Büchner's play *Woyzeck* was written in the
   a. 1830s   b. 1890s   c. 1920s   d. 1940s

2. The vocal lines in *Wozzeck* include
   a. distorted folk songs   c. *Sprechstimme*
   b. speaking   d. all of the above

3. Which musical form provides the basis for the last act of *Wozzeck*?
   a. variations   b. military march   c. passacaglia   d. lullaby

4. Which of the following statements regarding Berg is untrue?
   a. He composed a great quantity of music in all forms.
   b. He synthesized traditional and twentieth-century elements.
   c. As in the music dramas of Wagner, there is a continuous musical flow within each act of his
      opera *Wozzeck*.
   d. He first attracted international attention with his opera *Wozzeck*.

VI-10. ANTON WEBERN

SELF-TEST Multiple-choice: Circle the answer that best completes each item.
1. Webern's melodic lines are
   a. "atomized" into two- or three-note fragments
   b. reinforced by frequent tutti unison passages
   c. folklike, with narrow ranges and frequent repetitions
   d. basically in major and minor keys

2. Webern's twelve-tone works contain many examples of
   a. long singing melodies   c. strict polyphonic imitation
   b. melodic and harmonic repetition   d. homophonic texture

3. The least important element in Webern's music is
   a. texture   b. tone color   c. dynamic level   d. tonality

4. Webern's Five Pieces for Orchestra are scored for
   a. a chamber orchestra of eighteen soloists   c. the traditional large romantic orchestra
   b. solo voice, chorus, and orchestra   d. mandolin, harmonium, and strings

5. Webern
   a. had little formal musical training
   b. taught himself piano and cello
   c. earned a doctorate in music history from the University of Vienna
   d. enjoyed frequent performances of his own music

VI-11. BÉLA BARTÓK

SELF-TEST Multiple-choice: Circle the answer that best completes each item.

1. Bartók's principal performing medium was
   - a. conducting
   - b. piano
   - c. violin
   - d. flute

2. Bartók evolved a completely individual style that fused folk elements with
   - a. changes of meter and a powerful beat
   - b. twentieth-century sounds
   - c. classical forms
   - d. all of the above

3. The melodies Bartók used in most of his works are
   - a. authentic folk melodies gathered in his research
   - b. original themes that have a folk flavor
   - c. reminiscent of nineteenth-century symmetrical themes
   - d. exclusively Hungarian and Rumanian folk tunes

4. Bartók's six string quartets are widely thought to be the finest since those of
   - a. Dmitri Shostakovich
   - b. Ludwig van Beethoven
   - c. Joseph Haydn
   - d. Igor Stravinsky

5. While remaining within the framework of a tonal center, Bartók often used
   _____ in his music.
   - a. harsh dissonances
   - b. polychords
   - c. tone clusters
   - d. all of the above

6. Bartók's Concerto for Orchestra
   - a. is his most popular work
   - b. received its title because it was written for an orchestra of virtuosi
   - c. is romantic in spirit because of its emotional intensity, memorable themes, and vivid contrasts of mood
   - d. all of the above

VI-12. CHARLES IVES

SELF-TEST Multiple-choice: Circle the answer that best completes each item.

1. *Putnam's Camp, Redding, Connecticut*, is a child's impression of
   a. a summer at camp
   b. a Fourth of July picnic
   c. a fishing trip
   d. army life in the war

2. Charles Ives's father was a(n)
   a. insurance salesman
   b. physician
   c. professional athlete
   d. bandmaster

3. After graduating from Yale, Ives
   a. went into the insurance business
   b. began teaching
   c. began playing the trumpet professionally
   d. went into professional athletics

4. During most of his lifetime, Ives's musical compositions
   a. were enthusiastically received in public performances
   b. were quickly published by a major firm
   c. accumulated in the barn of his Connecticut farm
   d. were sought after by musicians eager to perform them in public

5. Ives's music contains elements of
   a. revival hymns and ragtime
   b. patriotic songs and barn dances
   c. village bands and church choirs
   d. all of the above

6. *Putnam's Camp, Redding, Connecticut*, illustrates Ives's technique of quoting snatches of familiar tunes by presenting fragments of
   a. *Yankee Doodle*
   b. *The British Grenadiers*
   c. both a and b
   d. neither a nor b

7. Ives's large and varied output includes works in many genres, but not
   a. symphonies
   b. operas
   c. songs
   d. chamber music

8. *Putnam's Camp, Redding, Connecticut*, is a movement from Ives's
   a. *Three Places in New England*
   b. *Essays before a Sonata*
   c. *Concord* Sonata
   d. *The Unanswered Question*

VI-13. GEORGE GERSHWIN

SELF-TEST Multiple-choice: Circle the answer that best completes each item.
1. Gershwin left high school at the age of fifteen to
   a. become a pianist demonstrating new songs in a publisher's salesroom
   b. study theory and composition in Paris
   c. work in his father's store
   d. develop his athletic talents

2. The Gershwin song that became a tremendous hit in 1920 was
   a. *La, La, Lucille*   c. *Swanee*
   b. *I Got Rhythm*   d. *Embraceable You*

3. *Porgy and Bess* is a(n)
   a. Broadway musical   c. rhapsody for piano
   b. opera   d. popular song

4. In addition to his musical skills, George Gershwin showed talent as a
   a. lyricist   c. sculptor
   b. clarinetist   d. painter

5. George Gershwin usually collaborated with the lyricist
   a. Jerome Kern   c. Paul Whiteman
   b. Irving Berlin   d. Ira Gershwin

6. Which of the following works is *not* by George Gershwin?
   a. *Of Thee I Sing*   c. *The Desert Song*
   b. *Porgy and Bess*   d. *An American in Paris*

7. *Rhapsody in Blue* opens with
   a. a solo flute   c. a muted trumpet
   b. the full orchestra   d. a solo clarinet

VI-14. WILLIAM GRANT STILL

SELF-TEST **Multiple-choice:** Circle the answer that best completes each item.

1. "Harlem Renaissance" was the name
   a. sometimes given to a flowering of African American culture during the years 1917-1935
   b. given to a housing project in New York City's Harlem
   c. of a city in Holland
   d. of a symphony by William Grant Still

2. William Grant Still's opera dealing with the Haitian slave rebellion is
   a. *Trouble in Tahiti*
   b. *Troubled Island*
   c. *Emperor Jones*
   d. *Once on this Island*

3. As a result of his studies in composition with composers from two opposing musical camps, the conservative George Whitefield Chadwick and the modernist Edgard Varèse, Still
   a. composed in a very conservative style
   b. composed in a highly dissonant style.
   c. composed in a mixture of conservative and avant-garde styles
   d. turned away from avant-garde styles and wrote compositions with a uniquely African American flavor.

4. Each movement of William Grant Still's *Afro-American Symphony* is prefaced by lines from a poem by
   a. Paul Laurence Dunbar
   b. Zora Neale Hurston
   c. W. E. B. DuBois
   d. James Weldon Johnson

5. William Grant Still's works in African American style, such as his *Afro-American Symphony*, were
   a. never performed during his lifetime
   b. severely criticized by audiences and critics
   c. panned by critics, but popular with audiences
   d. performed to critical acclaim in New York

6. After serving in the navy and a brief return to studies at Oberlin College, William Grant Still moved to New York where he
   a. made band arrangements and played in the orchestras of all-black musical shows
   b. practiced medicine
   c. served as a navy recruiter
   d. composed full time to satisfy his many commissions

VI-15. AARON COPLAND

SELF-TEST Multiple-choice: Circle the answer that best completes each item.
1. Copland's name has become synonymous with American music because of his use of
   a. revival hymns, cowboy songs, and other folk tunes
   b. jazz, blues, and ragtime elements
   c. subjects from American folklore
   d. all of the above

2. Copland's turn toward simplicity in the 1930s can be traced in part to
   a. the great depression   c. the influence of Schoenberg
   b. dissatisfaction with his own style   d. the influence of religion

3. In 1921 Copland began a three-year period of study in
   a. Germany   b. Austria   c. Italy   d. France

4. Which of the following works was *not* composed by Copland?
   a. *Concord* Sonata   c. *Billy the Kid*
   b. *Rodeo*   d. *Music for the Theater*

5. In addition to his compositions, Copland made valuable contributions to music
   in America by
   a. directing composer's groups   c. organizing concerts of American music
   b. writing books and magazine articles   d. all of the above

6. In 1925, and for a few years afterward, Copland's music showed the influence of
   a. impressionism   c. neobaroque styles
   b. jazz   d. expressionism

7. An example of Copland's use of serialist technique is
   a. *Music for the Theater*   c. *Fanfare for the Common Man*
   b. *Connotations for Orchestra*   d. *Appalachian Spring*

8. *Appalachian Spring* originated as a
   a. program symphony   c. ballet score
   b. song cycle   d. chamber opera

9. Copland depicted "Scenes of daily activity for the Bride and her Farmer-husband" in
   Appalachian Spring through
   a. five variations on the Shaker melody *Simple Gifts*
   b. intensely dissonant passages and humorous offbeat accents
   c. strings softly singing a hymnlike melody
   d. a joyful dance tune that is American in flavor

BIOGRAPHICAL SKETCH An American composer: _____

Born (year, place):
Died (year, place):

Personal life:

    family:

    health and physiognomy:

    personality:

Career:

    significant places:

    significant people:

    employers or patrons:

    means of making a living:

    financial situation:

Music:
    style of composition:

    general characteristics:

Output (List some of the major forms in which the composer worked, including the approximate
number of compositions if significant. List some of the major compositions in each category,
check those which you have heard, and circle those which you have studied):

Category:_____   _____   _____

Works:

Category:_____   _____   _____

Works:

VI-16. MUSICAL STYLES SINCE 1945

BASIC TERMS:

serialism   minimalist music   quotation music
chance music (aleatoric music)   microtone

SELF-TEST Multiple-choice: Circle the answer that best completes each item.
1. Minimalist music is characterized by
   a. the development of musical materials through random methods
   b. rapidly changing dynamics and textures
   c. a steady pulse, clear tonality, and insistent repetition of short melodic patterns
   d. the use of twelve-tone techniques to organize the dimensions of music

2. Many composers since the mid-1960s have made extensive use of quotations from earlier
   music as an attempt to
   a. simplify writing original compositions
   b. improve communication between the composer and the listener
   c. capitalize on the popularity of earlier works
   d. continue and develop serialist techniques

3. A major composer associated with the serialist movement is
   a. Philip Glass   b. Milton Babbitt   c. George Crumb   d. Ellen Taaffe Zwilich

4. All of the following are major developments in music since 1950 *except* the
   a. spread of chance music
   b. increased use of the twelve-tone system
   c. continued composition of symphonies in the classical style
   d. composition of music in which tone color, texture, dynamics, and rhythm are as important as
      pitch

5. Intervals smaller than the half step are called
   a. quartertones   b. tone clusters   c. macrotones   d. microtones

6. Twelve-tone compositional techniques used to organize rhythm, dynamics, tone color, and
   other dimensions of music to produce totally controlled and organized music are called
   a. chance music   b. minimalism   c. serialism   d. *Klangfarbenmelodie*

7. In chance or aleatoric music, the composer
   a. writes a rhythmic pattern but leaves it to the performer to determine the actual pitches
   b. takes a chance on which performers will perform the work
   c. chooses pitches, tone colors, and rhythms by random methods
   d. writes the music in a traditional manner, but allows the recording engineer to make changes

EXERCISE An overview of musical developments since 1945:

The text gives ten major developments in music since 1945. Identify the characteristics that differentiate each from the others, and name some of the major figures with representative compositions in each style.

1. Increased use of the *twelve-tone system*
   Characteristics:
   Special techniques:

   Composers and compositions:

2. *Serialism*—use of twelve-tone system techniques to organize rhythm, dynamics, and tone color
   Characteristics:
   Special techniques:

   Composers and compositions:

3. *Chance music*, in which a composer chooses pitches, tone colors, and rhythms by random methods, or allows a performer to choose much of the musical material
   Characteristics:
   Special techniques:

   Composers and compositions:

4. *Minimalist music*, characterized by a steady pulse, clear tonality, and insistent repetition of short melodic patterns
   Characteristics:
   Special techniques:

   Composers and compositions:

5. Works containing deliberate *quotations* from earlier music
   Characteristics:
   Special techniques:

   Composers and compositions:

MUSICAL STYLES SINCE 1945 (cont.)

6. A *return to tonality*
   Characteristics:
   Special techniques:

   Composers and compositions:

7. *Electronic music*
   Characteristics:
   Special techniques:

   Composers and compositions:

8. *"Liberation of sound"* — greater exploitation of noiselike sounds
   Characteristics:
   Special techniques:

   Composers and compositions:

9. *Mixed media*
   Characteristics:
   Special techniques:

   Composers and compositions:

10. New concepts of *rhythm* and *form*
    Characteristics:
    Special techniques:

    Composers and compositions:

VI-17. MUSIC SINCE 1945: FOUR REPRESENTATIVE PIECES

SELF-TEST Multiple-choice: Circle the answer that best completes each item.

1. *Poème électronique* was designed for the 1958 Brussels World's Fair, and was composed in collaboration with the famous architect
   a. I. M. Pei   b. Walter Gropius   c. Le Corbusier   d. Frank Lloyd Wright

2. Ellen Taaffe Zwilich won the 1983 Pulitzer Prize for Music for her composition
   a. String Quartet   c. Symphony No. 1
   b. Double Quartet for Strings   d. Concerto for Piano and Orchestra

3. Which of the following is *not* true of the music of Philip Glass?
   a. It has a very fast rate of change.
   b. It has a very clear tonality.
   c. It has a steady driving pulse.
   d. Melodic and rhythmic passages are constantly repeated.

4. Around 1940, John Cage invented the prepared piano, a(n)
   a. electronic keyboard capable of producing many percussive sounds
   b. grand piano complete with flowers, candelabra, and elaborate decorations
   c. grand piano whose sound is altered by objects such as bolts, screws, rubber bands, pieces of felt, paper, and plastic inserted between the strings of some of the keys
   d. ensemble of percussion instruments

5. Philip Glass's *Einstein on the Beach* is a(n)
   a. song cycle   b. symphonic poem   c. Broadway musical   d. opera

6. Ellen Taaffe Zwilich's *Concerto Grosso 1985* is an example of
   a. total serialism   c. minimalism
   b. quotation music   d. chance music

7. *Ionisation*, the first important work for percussion ensemble, was composed by
   a. John Cage   b. Edgard Varèse   c. Philip Glass   d. Ellen Taaffe Zwilich

8. John Cage's best-known work for prepared piano, and one of his most widely performed works, is
   a. *Sonatas and Interludes*   c. *Imaginary Landscape No. 4*
   b. *4'33"*   d. *Daughters of the Lonesome Isle*

9. Philip Glass's *Einstein on the Beach* deals with
   a. Columbus' discovery of America   c. the Indian leader Mahatma Gandhi
   b. nuclear destruction   d. an ancient Egyptian pharaoh

BIOGRAPHICAL SKETCH A twentieth-century composer: _____

Born (year, place):
Died (year, place):

Personal life:

    family:

    health and physiognomy:

    personality:

Career:

    significant places:

    significant people:

    employers or patrons:

    means of making a living:

    financial situation:

Music:

    style of composition:

    general characteristics:

Output (List some of the major forms in which the composer worked, including the approximate
    number of compositions if significant. List some of the major compositions in each category,
    check those which you have heard, and circle those which you have studied):

Category:_____   _____   _____

Works:

Category:_____   _____   _____

Works:

RESEARCH PROJECT *Sic transit gloria mundi (Thus passes away the glory of this world):*

In 1896 Sir George Grove brought out the first edition of his *Dictionary of Music and Musicians*. Within its four volumes, he devoted eight pages to Louis Spohr, but only a page and a half to Johannes Brahms. He gave four and a half pages to Johann Dussek, but a mere quarter-page to Smetana. Dvořák received three pages, but not until the final Appendix. Tchaikovsky received less than a page. In *The New Grove Dictionary of Music and Musicians* (sixth edition, 1980) Tchaikovsky is given almost thirty pages. Brahms has thirty-five pages in the later edition, as contrasted with Spohr's six. These figures are not necessarily reliable indications of lasting fame, but they do give some indication of how difficult it is to assess contemporary composers.

Looking back over the composers studied in Part VI (The Twentieth Century), which of them do you feel is most significant today? Why? Do you feel that the same composer will be just as significant 100 years from now? If so, why? If not, why not? Is there perhaps an unknown today—another Brahms, for example—who will come and eclipse the glory presently accorded one of our leading composers?

RESEARCH PROJECT **Is art music alive and well in the twenty-first century? A survey:**

The United States seems to be a country of statistics and percentages. Compile some statistics of your own: just how much contemporary art music is actually performed in your area? Make a survey of all the concerts offered in a week—or as much time as you need to make a representative sampling—including professional, community, and university performances. Determine the percentage of contemporary music. Is it a healthy ratio? While you are at it, now that the bicentennial is long over, how much of that percentage is American music?

City (metropolitan area, etc.):

Survey begun:

Survey ended:

Sources consulted (newspapers, advertising flyers, radio broadcasts, magazine listings, etc.):

Number of concerts advertised:

Total number of compositions performed:

Number of twentieth-century works scheduled: Percentage:

Number of American works scheduled: Percentage:

Do you feel these are healthy percentages?

If not, what can you do to change them?

VI-18. JAZZ

BASIC TERMS:

jazz	12-bar blues	New Orleans style	bebop (bop)
call and response	subdominant	front line	cool jazz
ragtime	rhythm section	swing band	free jazz
blues	chorus	riff	jazz rock (fusion)

SELF-TEST Multiple-choice: Circle the answer that best completes each item.

1. Ragtime flourished in the United States
   - a. just before the Civil War
   - b. from the 1860s to about 1890
   - c. from the 1890s to about 1915
   - d. between the two world wars

2. A bebop performance generally began and ended with
   - a. a statement of the main theme by one or two soloists in unison
   - b. a statement of the main theme by the whole combo in unison
   - c. improvisational sections by the soloists
   - d. free sections by the rhythm instruments to set the beat and tempo

3. The "front line" of a Dixieland group included
   - a. cornet, clarinet, and trombone
   - b. drums, bass, and banjo
   - c. piano
   - d. all of the above

4. Cool jazz
   - a. was related to bop but was calmer and more relaxed in character
   - b. consisted of short pieces freely improvised
   - c. used traditional jazz instrumental combinations
   - d. all of the above

5. One of the most important solo instruments of the swing era was the
   - a. cornet
   - b. guitar
   - c. tuba
   - d. saxophone

6. Which of the following is *not* a characteristic of fusion?
   - a. The group typically includes acoustic instruments along with synthesizers, guitar, and bass.
   - b. The percussion section is smaller than in earlier jazz.
   - c. Rock rhythms and tone colors are combined with the jazz musician's improvisatory approach.
   - d. Acoustic instruments are often used with electric attachments that expand the range of tonal effects.

7. The most famous blues singer of the 1920s, known as the "empress of the blues," was
   - a. Bessie Smith
   - b. Nina Simone
   - c. Diana Ross
   - d. Mahalia Jackson

8. Bebop was
   - a. music with sophisticated harmonies and unpredictable rhythms
   - b. usually played by small jazz groups
   - c. meant for attentive listening, not dancing
   - d. all of the above

9. Two notable blues compositions are *Memphis Blues* and *St. Louis Blues*, by
   a. Bessie Smith
   b. William C. Handy
   c. Louis Armstrong
   d. King Oliver

10. Ragtime is
   a. a style of composed piano music
   b. generally in duple meter
   c. performed at a moderate march tempo
   d. all of the above

11. The most distinctive feature of New Orleans jazz was the
   a. use of a saxophone for playing the melody
   b. collective improvisation by the front line
   c. solo breaks by the rhythm instruments
   d. lack of syncopated melodies

12. The following can be said about free jazz:
   a. It disregarded regular forms and established chord patterns.
   b. It can be compared to chance music.
   c. It began in the early 1960s.
   d. All of the above are true.

13. Blues music is usually written in _____ time.
   a. 4/4   b. 3/4   c. 6/8   d. 2/4

14. Short repeated melodic phrases frequently used during the swing era are called
   a. riffs   b. breaks   c. gigs   d. tags

15. The "king of ragtime" is acknowledged to be
   a. John Philip Sousa
   b. Bessie Smith
   c. Scott Joplin
   d. Louis Armstrong

16. In bebop, the beat of the music was mainly marked by the
   a. piano
   b. bass drum
   c. pizzicato bass
   d. trumpet

17. Duke Ellington was perhaps the most important composer, arranger, and conductor of the
   _____ era(s).
   a. swing   b. ragtime   c. bebop   d. all of the above

18. A major figure in the development of jazz rock or fusion was
   a. Miles Davis
   b. Ornette Coleman
   c. Louis Armstrong
   d. Stan Getz

19. The chord progression usually used in the blues involves only three basic chords: tonic, dominant, and
   a. supertonic   b. mediant   c. subdominant   d. submediant

20. Which of the following is *not* associated with cool jazz?
   a. Ornette Coleman
   b. Lennie Tristano
   c. Stan Getz
   d. Miles Davis

EXERCISE Roots of jazz:

Early jazz blended elements from many musical cultures, including west African, European, and American. Identify those musical practices and traditions in the following cultures that can be considered influences on early jazz.

West African:

Black African American:

European:

White European American:

Other:

EXERCISE Blues lyrics:

The text describes blues lyrics as several three-line stanzas, with the second line a repeat of the first. Other writers describe blues lyrics as a rhymed couplet in iambic pentameter (._._._._._), with the first line repeated. Whichever way you think of it, write a few stanzas that could serve as lyrics for vocal blues. As you try your luck, remember that most actual blues songs were improvised on the spot by the great performers.

EXERCISE Jazz styles:
The text discusses six of the most important styles in the history of jazz. Listen to representative examples of each style, and identify the characteristic features of that style.

1. New Orleans style

   Title:
   Date:

   Performers:

   Instrumentation:

   Similarities:

   Differences:

2. Swing

   Title:
   Date:

   Performers:

   Instrumentation:

   Similarities:

   Differences:

3. Bebop

   Title:
   Date:

   Performers:

   Instrumentation:

   Similarities:

   Differences:

4. Cool jazz

    Title:
    Date:

    Performers:

    Instrumentation:

    Similarities:

    Differences:

5. Free jazz

    Title:
    Date:

    Performers:

    Instrumentation:

    Similarities:

    Differences:

6. Jazz rock (fusion)

    Title:
    Date:

    Performers:

    Instrumentation:

    Similarities:

    Differences:

VI-19. THE AMERICAN MUSICAL

BASIC TERM:
musical (musical comedy)

Matching: Match each term to its definition.

1. the main section of a musical comedy song

2. type of theater that fuses script, acting, and spoken dialog with music, singing, and dancing, and with scenery, costumes, and spectacle

3. the introductory section of a musical comedy song

4. a variety show without a plot but with a unifying idea

5. musical theater work that combines song, spoken dialog, and dance with sophisticated musical techniques

6. a variety show with songs, comedy, juggling, acrobats, and animal acts, but no plot

a. chorus

b. musical

c. operetta

d. revue

e. vaudeville

f. verse

SELF-TEST Multiple choice: Circle the answer that best completes each item.

7. Leonard Bernstein was a well-known
   a. conductor
   b. author-lecturer
   c. composer of orchestral and vocal works
   d. all of the above

8. *Slaughter on Tenth Avenue*, the ballet used in the climax of *On Your Toes*, was choreographed by
   a. Stephen Sondheim
   b. Mikhail Baryshnikov
   c. George Balanchine
   d. Agnes de Mille

9. *West Side Story*
   a. is loosely based on Shakespeare's *Romeo and Juliet*
   b. is set in the slums of New York
   c. deals with the conflict between gang rivalry and youthful love
   d. all of the above

10. The lyrics for *West Side Story* were written by
    a. Oscar Hammerstein II
    b. Stephen Sondheim
    c. Jerome Robbins
    d. Leonard Bernstein

11. Which of the following is *not* a source of the American musical?
    a. operetta   b. oratorio   c. vaudeville   d. revue

12. Which of the following American musicals is *not* by Stephen Sondheim?
    a. *Sweeney Todd*
    b. *Of Thee I Sing*
    c. *Sunday in the Park with George*
    d. *Company*

RESEARCH PROJECT Musical theater:
   A little advance preparation can greatly enhance your appreciation and enjoyment of any trip to the theater, whether for opera, operetta, ballet, or musical comedy. Either on your own or as part of a class project, begin preparing for such a visit.

Name of the musical:

Composer: Lyricist:

Historical time: Place:

Comic or tragic:

Main characters:

Summary of plot, argument, or concept:

High points to look and listen for:

"Hit tunes":

VI-20. ROCK

BASIC TERM:
rock

SELF-TEST Matching: Match each term with its definition.

1. country and western

2. heavy metal

3. Motown

4. rhythm and blues

5. rap

6. reggae

7. rock

8. soul

a. dance music of African Americans that fused blues, jazz, and gospel styles

b. folklike, guitar-based style associated with rural white Americans

c. a style of rock music from the West Indies

d. vocal music with a hard, driving beat, often featuring electric guitar accompaniment and heavily amplified sound

e. basic rock with sexually explicit lyrics, bizarre costumes, and tremendous volume

f. emphasis on emotionality, gospel roots, and relationship to the black community

g. blend of rhythm and blues with popular music

h. rhythmic talking accompanied by recordings creating a collage of rhythmic effects

SELF-TEST Multiple-choice: Circle the answer that best completes each item.

9. A typical rock group consists of
    a. sections of brass, reeds, and percussion (rhythm)
    b. vocalist, two acoustic guitars, harmonica, and drums
    c. two electric guitars, electric bass, percussion, and electric keyboard
    d. vocalist, backup singers, and drums

10. The Beatles's influence on American rock music may be seen through later performer's use of
    a. "classical" and nonwestern instruments
    b. unconventional chord progressions
    c. new electronic and instrumental sounds
    d. all of the above

11. The harmonic progressions of rock are usually
    a. limited to only two chords
    b. the same as earlier popular music
    c. quite simple
    d. extremely complex

12. Rock is based on a powerful beat in quadruple meter with strong accents on _____ of each bar.
    a. the second and fourth beats
    b. the first and third beats
    c. the first beat
    d. all four beats

13. A method of singing used by males to reach notes higher than their normal range is called
    a. freaky   b. Yeah! Yeah!   c. disco   d. falsetto

14. The dominant dance music of the 1970s was
    a. the twist   b. the mashed potato   c. the bunny hop   d. disco

15. Which of these recordings can be considered a unified song cycle?
    a. the "white album"   c. *Magical Mystery Tour*
    b. *Sgt. Pepper's Lonely Hearts Club Band*   d. *Abbey Road*

16. Which of the following was not a member of the Beatles?
    a. John Lennon   b. Paul McCartney   c. George Harrison   d. Bob Dylan

RESEARCH PROJECT The diversity of rock styles—an analysis:
    The text stresses the enormous variety of rock styles. A major factor in this diversity is the tendency of rock to absorb elements and sounds from other styles, including folk music, country music, jazz, Latin music, western art music ranging from the Renaissance to avant-garde movements, and traditional music from Asia. Choose four popular rock pieces that show a definite relationship to other styles of music, identify these influences, and analyze the resulting combination.

1. Title:

    Performers: Style:

    Influenced by:

    Characteristics of the influencing style present in the piece:

    Result:

2. Title:

    Performers: Style:

    Influenced by:

    Characteristics of the influencing style present in the piece:

    Result:

3. Title:

    Performers: Style:

    Influenced by:

    Characteristics of the influencing style present in the piece:

    Result:

4. Title:

    Performers: Style:

    Influenced by:

    Characteristics of the influencing style present in the piece:

    Result:

BIOGRAPHICAL SKETCH A performer or composer of jazz or rock: _____

Born (year, place):
Died (year, place):

Personal life:

    family:

    health and physiognomy:

    personality:

Career:

    significant places:

    significant people:

    employers or patrons:

    means of making a living:

    financial situation:

Music:

    style of composition:

    general characteristics:

Output (List some of the major styles in which this person worked, including groups in which he or she performed. List some of the major compositions in each style, check those which you have heard, and circle those which you have studied):

Style:_____   _____

Works/recordings:

Style:_____   _____

Works/recordings:

RESEARCH PROJECT Some popular rock groups today. A comparison:

Choose four rock groups popular today. List the instrumentation, lead singers, and instrumentalists who also sing in each group. Describe and contrast any theatrical means employed, such as costumes, staging, or special effects. Identify the musical characteristics of each group, and describe how the groups are similar to and different from each other. When you have completed this analysis, what trends, if any, do you find in contemporary rock? Is rock in the process of forming a standardized instrumentation, such as the string quartet or swing's "big" band?

Group 1:
    Lead vocalists:

    Instrumentation (names and instruments; circle those who also sing):

    Theatrical aspects:
    Musical characteristics:

Group 2:
    Lead vocalists:

    Instrumentation:

    Theatrical aspects:

    Musical characteristics:

Group 3:
    Lead vocalists:

    Instrumentation:

    Theatrical aspects:

    Musical characteristics:

Group 4:
    Lead vocalists:

    Instrumentation:

    Theatrical aspects:

    Musical characteristics:

TRENDS:

Name_____

Class/section_____Date_____

Matching Match each composition with its composer:

a. Béla Bartók	1. *The Rite of Spring*	1._____
b. Alban Berg	2. *Appalachian Spring*	2._____
c. Leonard Bernstein	3. *A Survivor from Warsaw*	3._____
d. Aaron Copland	4. *Prelude to "The Afternoon of a Faun"*	4._____
e. Claude Debussy	5. *West Side Story*	5._____
f. George Gershwin	6. *Putnam's Camp, Redding, Connecticut*	6._____
g. Charles Ives	7. *Concerto Grosso 1985*	7._____
h. Arnold Schoenberg	8. *Afro-American Symphony*	8._____
i. William Grant Still	9. *Pierrot Lunaire*	9._____
j. Igor Stravinsky	10. *Wozzeck*	10._____
k. Anton Webern	11. Concerto for Orchestra	11._____
l. Ellen Taaffe Zwilich	12. *Rhapsody in Blue*	12._____

Multiple-choice: Choose the answer that best completes each item.

13. Placing one traditional chord against another at the same time, a technique of twentieth-century music, is known as
  a. a tone cluster   b. a polychord   c. polytonality   d. bitonality   13._____

14. The complete rejection of a tonal center, or treating each of the twelve tones as of equal importance, is called
  a. expanded tonality   c. atonality
  b. polytonality   d. modality   14._____

15. The main section of a musical comedy song is called the
  a. chorus   c. release
  b. verse   d. all of the above   15._____

16. The technique of using two or more tonal centers at the same time is called
  a. expanded tonality   c. atonality
  b. polytonality   d. twelve-tone   16._____

17. *Ostinato* refers to a
  a. rapid slide through different pitches
  b. chord made of tones only a half step or whole step apart
  c. combination of two traditional chords sounding together
  d. motive or phrase that is repeated persistently at the same pitch
     throughout a section   17._____

18. A variety show without a plot but with a unifying idea is called
  a. vaudeville   b. an operetta   c. a book musical   d. a revue   18._____

Unit Quiz VI, part 1, page 2 (cont.)

19. There are _____ different tones in the whole-tone scale.
    a. five
    b. six
    c. eight
    d. ten
    19._____

20. Which of the following characteristics is not usually associated with impressionism?
    a. evocation of mood
    b. clearly delineated forms
    c. suggestion
    d. symbolism
    20._____

21. The years from about _____ are generally considered the golden age of the American musical.
    a. 1890 to 1915
    b. 1905 to 1925
    c. 1920 to 1960
    d. 1960 to 1990
    21._____

22. Distortion is a technique used primarily in the _____ period.
    a. impressionist
    b. classical
    c. expressionist
    d. romantic
    22._____

23. A variety show with songs, comedy, juggling, acrobats, and animal acts, but no plot, is called
    a. vaudeville
    b. an operetta
    c. a revue
    d. a concept musical
    23._____

24. An eerily expressive kind of declamation midway between song and speech, introduced by the expressionist composers, is
    a. *Pierrot Lunaire*
    b. *stile rappresentativo*
    c. a cappella
    d. *Sprechstimme*
    24._____

Matching: Match each "ism" with its definition.

a. expressionism

b. impressionism

c. minimalism

d. neoclassicism

e. primitivism

f. serialism

25. music characterized by its steady pulse, clear tonality, and insistent repetition of short melodic fragments
25._____

26. deliberate evocation of unsophisticated power through insistent rhythms and percussive sounds
26._____

27. artistic movement, centered in Germany and Austria from 1905 to 1925, that stressed intense, subjective emotion
27._____

28. artistic movement from about 1920 to 1950 that is marked by emotional restraint, balance, and clarity
28._____

29. use of the technique of the twelve-tone system to organize rhythm, dynamics, and tone color
29._____

30. artistic movement, centered in France in the late nineteenth and early twentieth centuries, that stressed atmosphere, fluidity, and color
30._____

Name_____

Class/section_____Date_____

Matching: Match each style with its definition.

a. bebop

b. blues

c. cool jazz

d. country and
   western

e. free jazz

f. fusion

g. Motown

h. New Orleans
   style

i. ragtime

j. rhythm and
   blues

k. rock

l. soul

m. swing

1. piano style generally in duple meter, performed at a moderate march tempo, popular from the 1890s to about 1915   1._____

2. folklike, guitar-based style associated with rural white Americans   2._____

3. style that emerged in the early 1950s that was related to bop but calmer and more relaxed in character   3._____

4. style popular from 1935 to 1945, characterized by arrangements for about fifteen musicians   4._____

5. dance music of African Americans that fused blues, jazz, and gospel styles   5._____

6. combination of jazz improvisation with rock rhythms and tone colors   6._____

7. blend of rhythm and blues with popular music   7._____

8. style that emerged in the early 1960s that was not based on regular forms or established chord patterns   8._____

9. style that evolved in the early 1940s, characterized by complex rhythmic patterns, asymmetrical melodic phrases, solo improvisation, and irregular accents   9._____

10. form of vocal music usually characterized by a 12-bar chord progression over a steady 4/4 beat   10._____

11. style developed in the early 1900s, characterized by collective improvisation of solo performers over a clearly marked beat   11._____

12. vocal music with a hard, driving beat, often featuring electric guitar accompaniment and heavily amplified sound   12._____

13. emphasis on emotionality, gospel roots, and its relationship to the black community   13._____

Multiple-choice: Choose the answer that best completes each sentence.

14. The chord progression usually used in the blues involves only three basic chords: tonic, dominant, and

   a. supertonic   c. subdominant

   b. mediant   d. submediant   14._____

Unit Quiz VI, part 2, page 2

15. Early rock grew mainly out of _____, a dance music of African Americans that fused blues, jazz, and gospel styles.
    a. rhythm and blues   c. disco
    b. country and western   d. Motown   15._____

16. Frequently repeated short melodic phrases commonly used in swing are called
    a. riffs   b. breaks   c. gigs   d. tags   16._____

Matching: Match each performer with the style with which he or she is most closely associated:

a. bebop

b. blues

c. cool jazz

d. disco

e. folk rock

f. free jazz

g. Motown

h. New Orleans style

i. ragtime

j. rap

k. rhythm and blues

l. 1950s rock

m. soul

n. swing

17. Charlie "Bird" Parker   17._____
18. Louis Armstrong   18._____
19. Elvis Presley   19._____
20. Ornette Coleman   20._____
21. Donna Summer   21._____
22. Duke Ellington   22._____
23. Ice Cube   23._____
24. Miles Davis   24._____
25. Aretha Franklin   25._____
26. Benny Goodman   26._____
27. Diana Ross and the Supremes   27._____
28. Scott Joplin   28._____
29. Ella Fitzgerald   29._____
30. Stevie Wonder   30._____
31. Dizzy Gillespie   31._____
32. Glenn Miller   32._____
33. Chuck Berry   33._____
34. Bessie Smith   34._____
35. Ray Charles   35._____
36. Bob Dylan   36._____
37. Lester Young   37._____
38. W. C. Handy   38._____
39. Joseph "King" Oliver   39._____
40. Thelonious Monk   40._____

VII. NONWESTERN MUSIC

VII-1. MUSIC IN NONWESTERN CULTURES

BASIC TERMS:

membranophones   aerophones   heterophony

chordophones   idiophones

SELF-TEST Multiple-choice: Circle the answer that best completes each item.

1. Nonwestern music is most often transmitted
   a. orally from parent to child or teacher to student
   b. through the imitation of radio broadcasts
   c. through music notation
   d. all of the above

2. Nonwestern musical scales often contain _____ tones.
      a. five   b. six   c. seven   d. all of the above

3. A nasal, intense, and strained tone is cultivated by singers from
      a. Peru   c. the middle east and north Africa
      b. Siberia   d. sub-Saharan Africa

4. Which of the following statements is *not* true?
   a. Music of the nonwestern world is too varied to allow easy generalizations.
   b. Nonwestern traditions have been an important source of inspiration for twentieth-century western music.
   c. Improvisation is nonexistent in nonwestern music.
   d. Some composers in the nonwestern world combine traditional elements with western forms and styles.

SELF-TEST Matching: Match each term with its definition.

5. musical instrument whose sound generator is a stretched string   a. aerophone

6. musical instrument whose sound generator is a column of air   b. chordophone

7. musical instrument whose sound generator is a stretched skin or other membrane   c. idiophone

                                                              d. membranophone

8. musical instrument whose own material is the sound generator

RESEARCH PROJECT Other nonwestern musics:

There is such a wide variety of western and nonwestern music that ethnomusicologists speak of *musics* rather than implying there is one universal form or art of music. The text covers only a few of the main characteristics of this diversity in nonwestern music, and concentrates on two traditions: sub-Saharan Africa and the classical music of India. Other traditions, such as the musics of the near and middle east, Japan, China, southeast Asia, and the Native American, are not discussed.

Choosing one of the other nonwestern traditions, see if you can find characteristics in common with those of the traditions discussed (such as similarities in performance practices), unusual instruments, and other significant features. Be sure to include the names and numbers of those recordings you feel are representative of the style and you would recommend for use in a class discussion of the tradition you have chosen.

Culture:

Areas:

Forms:

Characteristics:

Instruments:

Performance characteristics:

Additional comments:

Recordings:

RESEARCH PROJECT Nonwestern instruments:

The text states "nonwestern instruments produce a wealth of sounds and come in many sizes, shapes, and materials." In order to experience some of these sounds, explore one culture, or one instrument type from each culture. Determine the correct category (see text) and describe the sound, shape, and use of the instrument.

AFRICA
drums
bimpombu, wana
azibwasi, sakala, towa
imbila, mbila, ilimba,
    marimba
mbira, sanza, kalimba
kora
kerar
bwanzi, ihango, dorungu,
    gwanzu

CARNATIC
mridanga
vïnä
tamburä

CHINA
ch'in
sheng
erh hu
p'i p'a
san hsien
chang ku

HINDUSTANI
sitär
tablä
saröd
tamburä

JAPAN
shakuhachi
samisen
koto
sho
biwa
tsuzumi

KOREA
komunko, hyon kum
taegum
haegum
chang go

NATIVE AMERICAN
drums
bull-roarer
axmäl
panpipes
whistles

NEAR AND MIDDLE EAST
üd
saz
rabäb
zurnä
naqqära
dawül

INSTRUMENT   CATEGORY   DESCRIPTION

VII-2. MUSIC IN SUB-SAHARAN AFRICA

BASIC TERM:
  call and response

SELF-TEST Multiple-choice: Circle the answer that best completes each item.
1. Drums in sub-Saharan Africa
      a. come in a wide variety of sizes, shapes, and forms
      b. are essential to many religious and political ceremonies
      c. are usually played in groups of two to four
      d. all of the above

2. Which of the following statements is *not* true with regard to sub-Saharan Africa?
      a. The most common type of instrument is the chordophone.
      b. The human body is often used as a percussion instrument.
      c. The people speak over 700 different languages.
      d. Music is usually performed outdoors.

3. Vocalists in Africa often use the _____ to accompany themselves.
      a. mbira   c. xylophone
      b. nose flute   d. pressure drum

4. A performance style in which the phrases of a soloist are repeatedly answered by those of a chorus
   is known as
      a. yodeling   c. polyphony
      b. call and response   d. campfire singing

5. The *mbira* may be described as a(n)
      a. hourglass-shaped drum
      b. melodic idiophone with tongues of metal or bamboo attached to a sounding board
      c. form of xylophone used in orchestras
      d. African form of string instrument

VII-3. CLASSICAL MUSIC OF INDIA

BASIC TERMS:
tambura   tala   tabla
raga   sitar

SELF-TEST Matching: Match each term with its definition.

1. alap

2. Hindustani music

3. Karnatak music

4. mridangam

5. raga

6. sitar

7. tabla

8. tala

9. tambura

10. vina

a. long-necked lute with four metal strings used to provide a
   continuous drone

b. pattern of notes used to create a melody

c. fretted long-necked plucked instrument with four melody and
   three drone strings, popular in south India

d. pair of single-headed drums played by one performer, popular
   in north India

e. music of south India, which developed more along its own lines

f. music of north India and Pakistan, which absorbed many
   Persian elements

g. rhapsodic introductory section of a composition

h. long-necked lute with seven strings, nine to thirteen sympathetically
   vibrating strings, and nineteen to twenty-three movable frets,
   popular in north India

i. repeated cycle of beats; a rhythmic pattern

j. two-headed barrel drum popular in south India

Name_____

Class/section_____ Date_____

Matching: Match each term with its definition.

a. membranophone in the shape of an hourglass capable of imitating human speech

b. musical instrument whose sound generator is a stretched string

c. pair of single-headed drums played by one performer, popular in north India

d. melodic idiophone with tongues of metal or bamboo attached to a sounding board

e. musical instrument whose sound generator is a column of air

f. musical instrument whose sound generator is a stretched skin or other membrane

g. musical instrument whose own material is the sound generator

h. texture in which instruments or voices perform the same basic melody but in versions that differ in ornamentation or rhythm

i. performance style in which the phrases of a soloist are repeatedly answered by those of a chorus

j. long-necked lute with seven strings, nine to thirteen sympathetically vibrating strings, and nineteen to twenty-three movable frets, popular in north India

1. aerophone   1._____

2. call and response   2._____

3. chordophone   3._____

4. heterophonic
   texture   4._____

5. idiophone   5._____

6. mbira   6._____

7. membranophone   7._____

8. pressure drum   8._____

9. sitar   9._____

10. tabla   10._____

Listening or essay question: To be provided by your instructor.

_____

_____

_____

_____

_____

APPENDIX:
GOING TO A CONCERT

BEFORE YOU GO:

Why go at all? With radio, television, and recordings all around us, why go to the expense and trouble of attending a live concert? For most people the answer is simple: recordings cannot duplicate the presence, quality, and range of live sound. Some performances must be seen as well as heard; some benefit from the interaction between performers and audience; some depend on the physical surroundings for subconscious and emotional involvement not possible through recorded sound. The fact that more concerts are given now than ever before indicates that audiences achieve pleasure and satisfaction from live performances. If you have not already discovered the reason for yourself, why not give it a try? The following comments are intended to help you achieve this goal as comfortably and easily as possible.

Choosing a concert: There are many kinds of concerts, and people quickly develop preferences, although the educated person should be familiar with the full range of possibilities. There are the symphonic orchestra and band concerts involving over 100 performers led by a conductor, and often with famous soloists. On a smaller scale there are chamber music concerts, involving one performer to each part, as in a piano trio, string quartet, woodwind quintet, brass or woodwind choir, or other chamber ensemble. Even smaller is the recital: a solo pianist, or any solo instrumentalist or vocalist, almost always with keyboard accompaniment. Musicals, operettas, operas, and ballets are all dramatic works and really must be seen to have their full impact. Then there are jazz, rock, and pop concerts where audiences frequently become actively involved in the performance.

Newspapers carry advertisements of coming events, especially in weekend sections. Radio stations frequently announce concerts; and college bulletin boards, especially around the offices of the music department, are usually crowded with announcements of professional, community, student, and amateur performances. Tickets should be obtained in advance (especially when seating is reserved), either at the box office, by mail, or through ticket services. Frequently there are student tickets or discounts for students, and one should not overlook the many free performances available in churches, colleges, and parks.

Preparation: A concert is an investment of time, effort, and money on your part. A little preparation will usually help you get the most satisfaction from the experience. Find out the program in advance, and read about the various pieces and composers represented (your text will be a good place to start). Try to listen to recordings of the works, especially if a foreign-language text is involved. Many public and college libraries have excellent record collections, some of which circulate. Information about works can frequently be found on record jackets, as well as in the program notes. In the case of a dramatic work such as an opera or ballet, some knowledge of the plot is essential. While a brief synopsis is published in the program, you may prefer the complete libretto or collections of synopses readily available in the library.

Dress: There was a time when one "dressed" for the opera or theater, which meant formal tuxedos and long evening dresses. Those days, except for special occasions, are long gone; but men often wear a coat and tie for Sunday and evening performances, and women wear the sort of outfit appropriate for going out to dinner. Other performances are normally less formal, and almost anything neat and clean is appropriate.

GOING TO A CONCERT (continued)

Punctuality: Plan to get to the concert hall or theater at least a half hour before the scheduled time of the performance. This will allow time for any last-minute emergencies, finding your seat, reading the program, and enjoying the ambience of the hall. It is not fair to let the people who were on time be distracted by latecomers, and so most concert halls and theaters today permit latecomers to take their seats only during logical breaks, such as the ends of compositions, scenes, or acts. Some halls have closed-circuit television for latecomers to watch while waiting, but imagine your disappointment if you arrive late for a one-act opera only to find that you will not be permitted to take your seat until the end of the act!

AT THE CONCERT:

The program: Most concerts and dramatic presentations will have a printed program that lists the works to be performed, the performers, program notes, and any other information that may be of value. The program is normally given to you by an usher, who will also help you find your seat. In the United States these services are usually provided without charge, but in Europe expect to purchase the program and tip the usher.

Listening: One may go to a concert for the gratification of all the senses, but music is still the art form dealing with sound. Good listening requires a great deal of mental effort, both intellectual and emotional. Naturally, any distractions, such as extraneous sounds, motions, movements, or behavior that interferes with the enjoyment of others, should be avoided. Save comments, foot tapping, humming, unwrapping candy, rustling of programs, and—if possible—even coughing for the intermission.

Applause: Audiences normally show their appreciation to a performer by applause (whistling, screaming, and hooting are quite impolite at most concerts). In order not to break the concentration of the performers and the audience, one generally does not applaud between movements of a symphony, sonata, suite, or any multimovement work. (In spite of this, opera audiences are notorious for breaking into enthusiastic applause after hit songs or arias, but one should at least wait until the music has stopped.) One usually applauds until the soloist or conductor reaches the wings of the stage, so as not to leave him or her walking off to silence. Applause by itself is simply a "thank you." It may range from polite but unenthusiastic through wildly vociferous to the electrifying rhythmic applause increasingly common in Europe. Calls of *bravo* may be heard (*brava* for a female performer; *bravi* for two or more performers), and sometimes even *encore*, which asks the performers to repeat a work or continue with one or more unscheduled compositions. If this is your first experience, just take your cue from the rest of the audience.

AFTER THE CONCERT:

Recordings: Your appreciation of a musical work, regardless of style, will increase through repeated hearings. If you enjoyed a work, listen to it again through recordings and relive the experience.

Concert reports: If the concert was an assignment, no doubt some form of report will be required. Some suggestions for writing a concert report and three simple forms follow, but your instructor will explain his or her specific requirements.

New experiences: We hope that your experience will have been a pleasant one, and that you will now be ready to try other possibilities, fully confident of your own *savoir faire*.

CONCERT REPORTS

SOME PRE-CONCERT SUGGESTIONS

1. Plan ahead; get your tickets early for best seating.
2. Reread these instructions just before attending the concert so you can direct your listening.
3. Save your program and ticket to attach to the concert report. You may wish to make a few notes on the program at the concert, but in general this is not necessary.
4. Write your report as soon after the concert as possible while the experience is still fresh in your mind.
5. When writing the report, use your program to remind yourself of what you heard.

WRITING THE CONCERT REPORT
(Please type if possible)

Your instructor will most likely give specific directions, and the outline that follows is only one of many possible. For example, your instructor may wish an essay discussion of all the works on a program (not just those you liked best and least), or some reference to the biographical details of the performers and/or soloists. The suggestions listed below are merely that, and may be adapted to suit your specific requirements. If you use a computer, be sure to run a spell-check program, and remember that even though this may be a music report, it should still reflect your abilities in proper writing techniques.

Paragraph 1. THE CONCERT ENVIRONMENT:
1. Describe the hall and physical surroundings.
2. Describe the behavior, dress, and general demeanor of the audience.
3. Describe the behavior, dress, and general demeanor of the performers.

Paragraph 2. THE MUSIC: the composition I liked *best* (if the concert consisted of one large work, choose the section or movement you liked best):
1. Title and composer.
2. Style (classic, romantic, etc.), and why you feel it is of that style.
3. Why you like this composition best.
4. Describe the music, considering some of the following points:
   Instrumentation: large or small orchestra, band, chorus, or chamber ensemble?
   Mood: peaceful, exciting, pompous? How did it make you feel? Emotions evoked?
   Programmatic or absolute? Did the music evoke any particular images or pictures in your mind?
   Texture: monodic, homophonic, polyphonic, or a combination?
   Harmony: major, minor, chromatic, modal, or combination? Consonant or Dissonant?
   Form (check concert program): sonata, ABA, rondo, minuet, scherzo?
   Rhythm, meter and tempo: fast, slow, changing? Syncopated?

Paragraph 3. THE PERFORMANCE: the composition I liked *best*:
1. How did it sound to you?
2. Was there sufficient energy (or calm) to bring across the music?
3. Were the performers playing or singing in tune?
4. Did the performers seem comfortable with the technical demands of the music?
5. Was there good ensemble and communication among the performers?
6. How did the conductor fulfill his/her role (if applicable)?

(Optional paragraph(s) on the composition (or movement) you liked almost as well, using the questions as above)

Paragraph 4. THE MUSIC: the composition I liked *least* (if the concert consisted of one large work, choose the section or movement you liked least):
  1. Title and composer.
  2. Style (classic, romantic, etc.), and why you feel it is of that style.
  3. What did you dislike about this composition?
  4. Describe the music: how did it make you feel? Did the music evoke any particular images or pictures in your mind? What emotions did the music evoke?

Paragraph 5. THE PERFORMANCE: the composition I liked *least*:
  1. How did it sound to you?
  2. Was there sufficient energy (or calm) to bring across the music?
  3. Were the performers playing or singing in tune?
  4. Did the performers seem comfortable with the technical demands of the music?
  5. Was there good ensemble and communication among the performers?
  6. How did the conductor fulfill his/her role (if applicable)?

Paragraph 6. General reactions to the experience of attending this concert:
  1. Was the experience new to you?
  2. How was it different from what you expected?
  3. Was it like or unlike other concerts you may have attended?
  4. Did you enjoy the experience?
  5. Would you recommend concertgoing to others?
  6. Would you go again if it weren't a requirement?

Remember to attach the ticket stub and program to your report.

Name_____

Class/section_____Date_____

CONCERT REPORT 1

Attach
ticket stub here,
and
program to back

1. Concert attended:

2. Date of concert:

3. Place of concert:

4. Type of concert (performing media):

5. General reaction to the concert environment:

6. Composition I liked best (if any) and why:

    title:

    composer:

    medium (if different from 4, above):

    movements:

    form:

    tempo:

    historical style:

    criticism of the musical work:

    criticism of the performance:

    overall reaction to this one work:

Concert Report 1 (cont.)

7. Composition I liked almost as well, and why:
   title:

   composer:

   medium (if different):

   movements:

   form:

   tempo:

   historical style:

   criticism of the music:

   criticism of the performance:

   overall reaction to this one work:

8. Composition I liked least (if any), and why:
   title:

   composer:

   medium (if different):

   movements:

   form:

   tempo:

   historical style:

   criticism of the music:

   criticism of the performance:

   overall reaction to this work:

9. Criticism and comments on the concert as a whole:

Name_____

Class/section_____Date_____

Attach
ticket stub here,
and
program to back

CONCERT REPORT 2

1. Concert attended:

2. Date of concert:

3. Place of concert:

4. Type of concert (performing media):

5. General reaction to the concert environment:

6. Composition I liked best (if any) and why:

   title:

   composer:

   medium (if different from 4, above):

   movements:

   form:

   tempo:

   historical style:

   criticism of the musical work:

   criticism of the performance:

   overall reaction to this one work:

Concert Report 2 (cont.)

7. Composition I liked almost as well, and why:
   title:

   composer:

   medium (if different):

   movements:

   form:

   tempo:

   historical style:

   criticism of the music:

   criticism of the performance:

   overall reaction to this one work:

8. Composition I liked least (if any), and why:
   title:

   composer:

   medium (if different):

   movements:

   form:

   tempo:

   historical style:

   criticism of the music:

   criticism of the performance:

   overall reaction to this work:

9. Criticism and comments on the concert as a whole:

Name_____

Class/section_____Date_____

CONCERT REPORT 3

Attach
ticket stub here,
and
program to back

1. Concert attended:

2. Date of concert:

3. Place of concert:

4. Type of concert (performing media):

5. General reaction to the concert environment:

6. Composition I liked best (if any) and why:

   title:

   composer:

   medium (if different from 4, above):

   movements:

   form:

   tempo:

   historical style:

   criticism of the musical work:

   criticism of the performance:

   overall reaction to this one work:

Concert Report 3 (cont.)

7. Composition I liked almost as well, and why:
    title:

    composer:

    medium (if different):

    movements:

    form:

    tempo:

    historical style:

    criticism of the music:

    criticism of the performance:

    overall reaction to this one work:

8. Composition I liked least (if any), and why:
    title:

    composer:

    medium (if different):

    movements:

    form:

    tempo:

    historical style:

    criticism of the music:

    criticism of the performance:

    overall reaction to this work:

9. Criticism and comments on the concert as a whole:

POST-COURSE LISTENING ANALYSIS

Think back to the very first lesson in the text, when you listened to the **Prelude to Act III of Richard Wagner's** *Lohengrin* for the first time. Listen to it once more, and again write your personal and emotional reactions to the work, and analyze the music and its technical aspects as completely and specifically as you can.

Now listen again to *C-Jam Blues* as performed by Duke Ellington and his orchestra. Compare it with the Wagner prelude, using the full range of your knowledge of music.

POST-COURSE EVALUATION What do you think?

Write a brief statement summarizing what, if anything, this course has done for you. Look back at the Pre-Course Questionnaire you completed at the beginning of your studies in music. Did you meet the goals you set at that time? Have your attitudes and tastes changed? Also, please give an evaluation of the course. For example, which topics pleased you; which topics did you like the least (detest?); what would you have liked to see more of and what less of; which pieces did you like best or least? Indicate anything, in other words, that would make the course more interesting and valuable for the students following you.

Thank you.

ANSWER KEY
FOR SELF-TEST QUESTIONS

I. ELEMENTS

I-1.   1-c, 2-a, 3-b, 4-a, 5-d, 6-c, 7-d, 8-b, 9-b, 10-a, 11-b, 12-d, 13-c, 14-c, 15-a

I-2.   1-a, 2-c, 3-d, 4-c, 5-b, 6-d, 7-b, 8-a, 9-d, 10-b, 11-d, 12-c, 13-d, 14-c, 15-a, 16-b, 17-b, 18-d, 19-c, 20-a

I-3.   1-c, 2-i, 3-h, 4-a, 5-b, 6-j, 7-d, 8-e, 9-f, 10-g, 11-m, 12-o, 13-s, 14-t, 15-l, 16-p, 17-r, 18-k, 19-q, 20-n

I-4.   1. BEAD, 2. CABBAGE, 3. DEAF, 4. BADGE, 5. CAGE, 6. FADE

I-5.   1-a, 2-c, 3-d, 4-b, 5-d, 6-c, 7-b, 8-a, 9-d, 10-b

I-6.   1-c, 2-a, 3-b, 4-a, 5-d, 6-b, 7-c, 8-d, 9-b, 10-a

I-7.   1-b, 2-a, 3-c, 4-d, 5-c

I-8.   1-d, 2-b, 3-c, 4-b, 5-c, 6-a, 7-d, 8-d, 9-c, 10-c

I-9.   1-d, 2-d, 3-a, 4-d, 5-b

I-10.   1-b, 2-a, 3-d

II. THE MIDDLE AGES AND RENAISSANCE

II-1.   1-a, 2-d, 3-a, 4-c, 5-b, 6-a, 7-c, 8-c, 9-d, 10-d, 11-b, 12-a, 13-d, 14-d, 15-b, 16-b, 17-a

II-2.   1-c, 2-c, 3-c, 4-b, 5-a, 6-b, 7-d, 8-d, 9-b, 10-a, 11-d, 12-c, 13-a, 14-d, 15-motet, mass; 16- Kyrie, Gloria, Credo, Sanctus, Agnus Dei; 17-a cappella; 18-four; 19-the overlapping of voices; 20-imitation

III. THE BAROQUE PERIOD

III-1. 1-major, minor; 2-Johann Sebastian Bach, George Frideric Handel; 3-basso continuo; 4-terraced dynamics; 5-movement; 6-b, 7-b, 8-d, 9-a, 10-d

III-2. 1-b, 2-d, 3-a, 4-d, 5-c

III-3. 1-three; 2-fast, slow, fast; 3-tutti; 4-ritornello; 5-flute, violin, harpsichord

III-4. 1-d, 2-e, 3-g, 4-f, 5-j, 6-h, 7-i, 8-a, 9-c, 10-b

III-5. 1-d, 2-b, 3-e, 4-g, 5-c, 6-j, 7-i, 8-a, 9-k, 10-l, 11-f, 12-h

III-6. 1-d, 2-a, 3-b, 4-d, 5-b, 6-a, 7-a

III-7.   1-c, 2-b, 3-a, 4-b, 5-a, 6-c

III-8.   1-basso ostinato; 2-*Aeneid*, girl's boarding school, the director was a dancing master, strings and harpsichord continuo; 3-Westminster Abbey

III-9.   1-c, 2-d, 3-c, 4-c, 5-c

III-10.   1-b, 2-d, 3-c, 4-d, 5-c, 6-a

III-11.   1-Leipzig; 2-aria, recitative; 3-*Art of the Fugue*; 4-harmony, polyphonic; 5-*The Well-Tempered Clavier*; 6-c, 7-c, 8-a, 9-d, 10-a

III-12.   1-a, 2-d, 3-b, 4-c, 5-a

III-13.   1-c, 2-d, 3-b, 4-b, 5-a

III-14.   1-c, 2-d, 3-b, 4-c, 5-b

III-15.   1-a, 2-a, 3-a, 4-b, 5-a, 6-b, 7-b, 8-b

IV. THE CLASSICAL PERIOD

IV-1.   Baroque: 1, 2, 5, 7, 8, 11, 12, 15, 19, 20
         Classical: 3, 4, 6, 9, 10, 13, 14, 16, 17, 18

IV-2.   1-a, 2-b, 3-a, 4-d, 5-d, 6-b, 7-a, 8-d, 9-b, 10-b

IV-3.   1-exposition, development, recapitulation; 2-introduction; 3-bridge; 4-coda; 5-motives; 6-Ludwig von Köchel, the man who catalogued Mozart's music in the nineteenth century; 7-c, 8-c, 9-a, 10-a, 11-c

IV-4.   1-b, 2-a, 3-b

IV-5.   1-c, 2-a, 3-b, 4-c, 5-d, 6-a, 7-d

IV-6.   1-d, 2-a, 3-d, 4-b, 5-c

IV-7.   1-d, 2-b, 3-a, 4-c, 5-a

IV-8.   1-a, 2-b, 3-c, 4-c, 5-d, 6-b

IV-9.   1-b, 2-b, 3-c, 4-c, 5-a, 6-d

IV-10.   1-Esterházy; 2-London; 3-string quartets, symphonies; 4-*The Seasons, The Creation*; 5-b, 6-d, 7-c

IV-11.   1-d, 2-b, 3-d, 4-a, 5-c, 6-c, 7-a, 8-a, 9-c, 10-c

IV-12.   1-vocal soloists, chorus; 2-musical sketchbooks; 3-*Fidelio*; 4-Napoleon, *Eroica*;
5-classical, romantic; 6-b, 7-d, 8-c, 9-c, 10-b

V. THE ROMANTIC PERIOD

V-1.   Classicism: 1, 2, 3, 8, 12, 14, 19, 20
Romanticism: 4, 5, 6, 7, 9, 10, 11, 13, 15, 16, 17, 18

V-2.   1-d, 2-b, 3-d, 4-a, 5-b, 6-French Revolution, Napoleonic Wars; 7-piano; 8-subscription;
9-New York Philharmonic; 10-Chicago, Cleveland, Boston, Oberlin, Philadelphia

V-3.   1-lied; 2-strophic; 3-through-composed; 4-Johann Wolfgang von Goethe, Heinrich Heine;
5-introduction, postlude, piano

V-4.   1-d, 2-a, 3-d, 4-b, 5-c, 6-c

V-5.   1-d, 2-d, 3-d, 4-b, 5-d

V-6.   1-d, 2-b, 3-d, 4-b, 5-a

V-7.   1-d, 2-d, 3-a, 4-a; 5-étude; 6-nocturne; 7-polonaise; 8-polonaises, mazurkas

V-8   1-a, 2-d, 3-d, 4-b, 5-c, 6-d, 7-b, 8-b, 9-a

V-9.   1-a, 2-b, 3-d, 4-c, 5-b

V-10.   1-e, 2-c, 3-d, 4-e, 5-b, 6-a, 7-e, 8-b, 9-b, 10-a, 11-d, 12-c, 13-a, 14-b, 15-b

V-11.   1-b, 2-d, 3-d, 4-d, 5-a, 6-c, 7-c, 8-a, 9-c, 10-a

V-12.   1-b, 2-c, 3-c, 4-b, 5-a, 6-a, 7-d

V-13.   1-d, 2-b, 3-a, 4-b, 5-c, 6-d

V-14.   1-b, 2-b, 3-b, 4-d, 5-b

V-15.   1-d, 2-b, 3-c, 4-d, 5-c

V-16.   1-d, 2-b, 3-c, 4-d, 5-d, 6-c, 7-d, 8-a, 9-b, 10-d

V-17.   1-d, 2-c, 3-b, 4-d, 5-d, 6-c, 7-d, 8-a, 9-b, 10-b

V-18.   1-b, 2-d, 3-d, 4-b, 5-a, 6-b, 7-d, 8-b, 9-d, 10-c

VI. THE TWENTIETH CENTURY

VI-1.   1-d, 2-d, 3-b, 4-b, 5-d, 6-d, 7-d, 8-a, 9-c, 10-d

VI-2.   1-b, 2-b, 3-a, 4-c, 5-a, 6-b, 7-b

VI-3   1-light, color, atmosphere; 2-Claude Debussy; 3-*Impression: Sunrise*; 4-musical, sonorous; 5-Paul Verlaine; 6-a, 7-c, 8-d, 9-a, 10-a

VI-4.   1-a, 2-b, 3-d, 4-c, 5-d, 6-a, 7-d, 8-d, 9-c

VI-5.   1-d, 2-a, 3-a, 4-c, 5-a, 6-b

VI-6.   1-a, 2-b, 3-c, 4-c, 5-c, 6-c, 7-a, 8-c, 9-d, 10-d

VI-7.   1-c, 2-b, 3-c, 4-d, 5-d, 6-b, 7-a, 8-b, 9-b, 10-b

VI-8.   1-d, 2-b, 3-b, 4-b, 5-b, 6-c

VI-9.   1-a, 2-d, 3-a, 4-a

VI-10.   1-a, 2-c, 3-d, 4-a, 5-c

VI-11.   1-b, 2-d, 3-b, 4-b, 5-d, 6-d

VI-12.   1-b, 2-d, 3-a, 4-c, 5-d, 6-c, 7-b, 8-a

VI-13.   1-a, 2-c, 3-b, 4-d, 5-d, 6-c, 7-d

VI-14.   1-a, 2-b, 3-d, 4-a, 5-d, 6-a

VI-15.   1-d, 2-a, 3-d, 4-a, 5-d, 6-b, 7-b, 8-c, 9-a

VI-16.   1-c, 2-b, 3-b, 4-c, 5-d, 6-c, 7-c

VI-17.   1-c, 2-c, 3-a, 4-c, 5-d, 6-b, 7-b, 8-a, 9-b

VI-18.   1-c, 2-a, 3-a, 4-a, 5-d, 6-b, 7-a, 8-d, 9-b, 10-d, 11-b, 12-d, 13-a, 14-a, 15-c, 16-c, 17-a, 18-a, 19-c, 20-a

VI-19.   1-a, 2-b, 3-f, 4-d, 5-c, 6-e, 7-d, 8-c, 9-d, 10-b, 11-b, 12-b

VI-20.   1-b, 2-e, 3-g, 4-a, 5-h, 6-c, 7-d, 8-f, 9-c, 10-d, 11-a, 12-a, 13-d, 14-d, 15-b, 16-d

VII. NONWESTERN MUSIC

VII-1.   1-a, 2-d, 3-e, 4-c, 5-b, 6-a, 7-d, 8-c

VII-2.   1-d, 2-a, 3-a, 4-b, 5-b

VII-3.   1-g, 2-f, 3-e, 4-j, 5-b, 6-h, 7-d, 8-i, 9-a, 10-c

NOTES

NOTES